FANNYE COOK

FANNYE COOK

Mississippi's Pioneering Conservationist

Dorothy Shawhan

Edited and with contributions by

Marion Barnwell and Libby Hartfield

University Press of Mississippi / Jackson

www.upress.state.ms.us

Publication of this book was made possible in part
by a generous donation from Wildlife Mississippi.

The University Press of Mississippi is a member
of the Association of American University Presses.

Manufactured in the United States of America

First printing 2018
∞

Library of Congress Cataloging-in-Publication Data

Names: Shawhan, Dorothy, author. | Barnwell, Marion, editor. | Hartfield, Libby, editor. |
Wildlife Mississippi (Organization), sponsor.
Title: Fannye Cook : Mississippi's pioneering conservationist / Dorothy Shawhan ; edited and
with contributions by Marion Barnwell and Libby Hartfield.
Description: Jackson : University Press of Mississippi, 2018. | "Made possible in part by a
generous donation from Wildlife Mississippi." |Includes bibliographical references and index. |
Identifiers: LCCN 2017021077 (print) | LCCN 2017027038 (ebook) | ISBN 9781496814135 (epub
single) | ISBN 9781496814142 (epub institutional) | ISBN 9781496814159 (pdf single) | ISBN
9781496814166 (pdf institutional) | ISBN 9781496814128 (cloth : alk. paper)
Subjects: LCSH: Cook, Fannye A. | Women conservationists—Mississippi—Biography. |
Conservationists—Mississippi—Biography. | Women naturalists—Mississippi—Biography. |
Naturalists—Mississippi—Biography.
Classification: LCC S926.C66 (ebook) | LCC S926.C66 S53 2018 (print) | DDC 333.72092
[B]—dc23
LC record available at https://lccn.loc.gov/2017021077

British Library Cataloging-in-Publication Data available

For Madeleine,
her cousins,
and their generation

Contents

Foreword

Even though Fannye Cook retired from the Mississippi Museum of Natural Science (MMNS) in 1958 and died in 1964, she was still a presence when I arrived as an employee in 1978 and she was a guiding inspiration through the thirty-seven years I spent as education coordinator and, later, as director. We museum staffers often speculated as to how she would have wanted things done, and whether she would have been pleased by what we were accomplishing or displeased if we were falling short of her mark. Bill Turcotte, who knew and worked for Miss Cook, assured us that while she was a demanding task master who set an example of striving for excellence, she was never unrealistic in her expectations.

Cook was a pioneer conservationist and scientist, and the driving force behind the creation of the Mississippi Game and Fish Commission (now called the Mississippi Department of Wildlife, Fisheries, and Parks) and the Mississippi Museum of Natural Science. In the 1920s she began the first comprehensive effort to collect and catalogue the plants and animals of Mississippi and continued this work until her death. She also led an extensive political grassroots effort to implement game laws and protect the state's natural environment.

For many decades before and during her tenure as director, she was the most widely known scientist in Mississippi and was the go-to person when anyone outside the state needed biological information or actual specimens from the state. Cook corresponded with Aldo Leopold, the father of wildlife ecology in North America, before his famed trip to Mississippi in 1928. Leopold traveled south to survey wildlife populations after surveying several northern states because he wanted to compare results in different habitats. He picked Mississippi out of curiosity about wildlife conditions in a state with no organized game and fish regulations. While he was here, he visited Cook in her Crystal Springs home. At Leopold's request, she edited his draft report, making comments and corrections through several letters with enough detail to include a discussion of Partridgeberry seeds.

She also knew and collaborated with Roger Conant, the foremost authority on reptiles and amphibians at that time, and he asked her to supply data concerning Mississippi reptiles. While serving as director of the zoo in Philadelphia, Pennsylvania, he even requested, on one occasion, that she send live snakes from Mississippi by train. She complied as if it were routine!

A book about Fannye Cook's critical role in establishing game and fish laws in Mississippi and preserving the state's native species and habitats had been discussed for years. When I mentioned the idea to Leila Salisbury at University Press of Mississippi, she recruited Dorothy Shawhan for the task. It took a team approach to identify contacts and supply the documents Dorothy needed. Unfortunately, many of the museum's historical archives had been soaked by Pearl River water during the flood of 1979; they were then dried and stored at the Mississippi Department of Archives and History. About half of the Fannye Cook archival materials, including hundreds of photographs, were unharmed and were retained by the Mississippi Museum of Natural Science. But because of the flood, all the documents were out of order and many were in poor condition.

Cook's astonishing life can never be wholly reconstructed from the business papers and letters available, but they tell us much about her professional side. Dorothy and I very much wanted to find more documentation of her personal life, but unfortunately much of that remains hidden. We know she was devoted to her large, loving family and there are family letters to verify that she kept in close contact with them through the years. Her family was fiercely loyal to her and worked with her often, particularly in the 1920s when she was working to persuade the state's leading citizens and the legislature to provide funds for a state department dedicated to wildlife. After the legislation was passed in 1932, Fannye's sister, Vivian, worked alongside her for years in the Plant and Animal Survey of the Works Progress Administration (WPA).

Dorothy's untimely death during the second draft of this book prevents us from knowing exactly how she would have dealt with the personal side of Cook's life in the final version. Marion Barnwell's willingness to finish the final draft helped make this book possible. Marion was Dorothy's close friend and spent many weeks poring over the manuscript and related documents, following leads, and tying up loose ends to bring a resolution to this biography. Dorothy's research documents and drafts for this book will be placed in the Delta State University archives in Cleveland as a starting point for future researchers.

From my own experience, I know that Cook also had a group of close friends with whom she traveled and bird-watched. I was fortunate to get to know several of those friends during the last years of their lives and to hear small bits and pieces of their adventures together, but we found no letters between Cook and these friends to inform us as to their daily lives and personal feelings. In the mid-seventies, before I came to work at the MMNS, I had the pleasure of bird-watching with Frances Wills, Evelyn Tackett, and the Berry sisters, Christine and Mary, in the woods that now comprise the natural area behind the MMNS in LeFleur's Bluff State Park. They were kind and patient ladies but determined to find the birds they wanted to see that morning and worked diligently until they were satisfied they knew what birds were in those woods. I believe Cook would have been very much like them.

One day in 1988, soon after I was named director of the museum, Frances Wills visited me in the museum to offer her congratulations and support, and identified herself as "Fannye's best friend and birding buddy." Bebe Wolfe and Evelyn Tackett confirmed this close friendship, and Evelyn donated the spotting scope Cook used on birding trips for many years. It had been passed to Frances Wills when Cook died and then to Evelyn when Frances could no longer use it. The scope is now on display in the museum's "Cook exhibit," *History of the Museum*.

Family members have been fiercely loyal to her and extremely supportive of the museum since her death. Great nephew Bill Cook is present for many public events in the museum, and great niece Mary Elizabeth Smith visits often with her grandchildren.

Even as we prepare to go to press with this manuscript, friends approach Marion and me with stories of Cook that we feel compelled to document. Dick Hall, Mississippi highway commissioner and longtime Mississippi state senator, recalls meeting Fannye Cook when he was a young boy. He and his friends had ridden their bikes to the Wildlife Museum that was located on the present site of University Hospital. He remembers that she was eager to share her knowledge and content to let the boys wander through the exhibits and spend time examining the taxidermy specimens. Veterinarian Dr. Troy Majure remembers visiting Cook's office and museum exhibits with his mother, who was a friend of Cook's as well as a naturalist and bird watcher. Many people in Crystal Springs have fond memories of the Cook sisters and tell stories of how Fannye Cook attracted wildlife to her gardens.

Her legacy lives on. The Department of Wildlife, Fisheries, and Parks has been successful in restoring populations of many species of native wildlife that might have been eliminated from the state had Cook not educated people and lobbied for conservation measures in the 1930s. Thousands of acres of prime natural habitat have been conserved and enjoyed by millions of people over the past eighty-five years through initiatives started by Fannye Cook. Her publications are still relevant to science, and, until very recently, her book *Freshwater Fishes in Mississippi* was used as the textbook for the study of fishes in all our state colleges and universities. The Mississippi Museum of Natural Science has expanded to a large institution with conservation biologists on staff who continue to research and monitor the state's plants and animals and their habitats, with emphasis on rare and endangered species. The biological collections Cook started through the WPA project have grown to more than a million specimens and are used frequently by scientists. The museum's exhibits, aquariums, and educational programs serve more than 150,000 visitors each year. These visitors, many of whom are children, have been unknowingly affected by Fannye Cook. Certainly she would be gratified to know her life's work continues and that her love of nature has been passed on to so many people.

On November 2, 2016, thanks to the Mississippi Department of Transportation and Wildlife Mississippi, a three-thousand-acre tract of land on the Pearl River was set aside for public use and named Fannye Cook Natural Area in her honor.

Both a biography and a history, this book is a portrait of a patient, determined woman who changed the world for all of us by conserving the natural world of Mississippi.

—Libby Hartfield

Preface

Imagine the wholesale destruction of natural habitats and wildlife that Fannye Cook witnessed in the early 1900s. Impenetrable Delta forests and the towering pinelands of south Mississippi were stripped bare. The blackland prairie of northeast Mississippi was farmed to the point that less than one percent of it remains today. White-tailed deer, Louisiana black bear, American alligator, wood duck, and other species were nearly eliminated by lawless exploitation. Streams and rivers were choked with eroding soil. The idea of caring for the land and its community of inhabitants, what writer and ecologist Aldo Leopold would later call a "land ethic," had not taken hold in Mississippi.

Fannye Cook, perhaps more than any other Mississippian before or since, sought to change that. She petitioned to make wildlife conservation a moral responsibility. In fact, she dedicated her life to this effort.

Wildlife Mississippi is truly honored to underwrite the publication of this book. Miss Cook's accomplishments are unknown to most Mississippians, and *Fannye Cook: Mississippi's Passionate Conservationist* will help all of us get to know her better.

Wildlife Mississippi feels a deep sense of responsibility to continue Miss Cook's work in conserving our state's natural heritage, so it may be cherished and enjoyed by generations to come. More than a half century after her death, we are still repairing the damage Miss Cook observed.

We have made notable progress since Wildlife Mississippi was formed twenty years ago by protecting, restoring, and enhancing nearly 450,000 acres of land in the state. We have achieved this by working with a community of like-minded people, private landowners, other organizations, and government agencies. We believe that a clean environment and functioning natural systems can help make our economy healthy. After all, Wildlife Mississippi's vision statement is "The conservation of Mississippi's lands, waters, and natural heritage will secure the state's quality of life by making it a better place to live, work, and raise a family."

Nowhere is that linkage more apparent than in the Mississippi Delta, where Wildlife Mississippi began its work. There, groundwater is being withdrawn for irrigation faster than it can be replenished. Nothing less than the future of one of the world's richest agricultural economies is at stake.

With 80 percent of Americans now living in urban areas—and farther from natural spaces—our challenge now is to help people maintain enough of a connection to the natural world to care about it and see it as essential to their well-being. Thanks to Miss Cook, and those inspired by her, there are still places in Mississippi where nature is within reach and holding its ground. Horn Island, which Ms. Cook helped protect as part of what is now the Gulf Islands National Seashore, is about as wild as any place in America. The bottomland hardwood forests of the Mississippi River floodplain cover more than a million acres in Mississippi and neighboring states. The two-thousand-year-old giant bald cypress trees of Sky Lake rival the giant sequoia and redwoods of California. Rivers such as the Pascagoula, the Pearl, and the Buttahatchie and Bayou Pierre still harbor ancient species such as gulf sturgeon, walleye, alligator gar, and paddlefish, as well as turtles, fish, and mussels found nowhere else in the world.

Wildlife Mississippi is working in all these places and more. It is developing opportunities for Mississippians to discover and learn about the natural world close to home. The Fannye Cook Natural Area in the heart of greater Jackson is a twenty-six-thousand-acre tract along the Pearl River in Flowood dedicated to Miss Cook in November 2016. With more than eight hundred thousand people living within an hour's drive of Mississippi's largest urban natural area, we are now working to open it for public use for conservation education, walking, biking, paddling, nature photography, hunting, fishing, and other activities.

In addition to her work on this book, Libby Hartfield is working with Wildlife Mississippi to coordinate the development of trails and other amenities necessary to open the Fannye Cook Natural Area. For thirty-seven years, Hartfield served as director of the Mississippi Museum of Natural

Science, following in the wake of Miss Cook, who was the museum's first director.

Thankfully, many Mississippians value outdoor experiences—something Leopold recognized almost a hundred years ago. Today, more Mississippians than ever care about healthy wildlife populations and functioning natural systems. They believe, as Wildlife Mississippi does, that all of us share a responsibility to conserve these spaces for present and future generations. Our approach is to help people, especially private landowners, see that conservation makes common sense *as well as* economic sense. We do that by working with government agencies, policy leaders, and businesses to create incentives to protect water quality and conserve natural habitats.

Wildlife Mississippi believes that it is not enough to preach that all of us have an unquestionable responsibility to conserve the natural environment around us. We must also find ways to make it feasible and desirable. That's what Fannye Cook taught us through her selfless and steadfast actions to make Mississippi a better place to live, work, and raise a family.

To learn more about Wildlife Mississippi, see www.wildlifemiss.org.

—Wildlife Mississippi

Acknowledgments

Tremendous thanks to the Mississippi Department of Wildlife, Fisheries, and Parks, the Mississippi Museum of Natural Science, and staff (past and present) who helped pull together reference materials for this book. Tommy Shropshire, Cathy Carter Shropshire, and Will McDearman saved so many of Fannye Cook's precious biological specimens from the flood waters in 1979, when the Mississippi Museum of Natural Science building on Jefferson Street was inundated by four feet of water. Mary Stevens Stripling was the museum librarian and worked diligently to dry out many of Fannye Cook's letters and documents that were briefly under water. Stripling archived the Fannye Cook collection, compiled the bibliography, and provided research documents to us. Bill Stripling put in many hours to digitize and restore the archival photographs used in this book. Laura Heller at the Mississippi Department of Archives and History was also very helpful.

Thanks to Suzanne Marrs for the terrific material from Eudora Welty's letters, and to the family of Fannye Cook for letters and remembrances. Special thanks to Alan Huffman, Charles Knight, Angel Rohnke, Matt Roberts, Heather Sullivan, Megan Fedrick, and Nick Winstead for all their help. And thanks to Leslie Griffin in Cleveland, Tommy Barnhardt in Crystal Springs, Martha Swain and Bridget Pieschel in Columbus, Dorothy Shawhan's sister Margaret Ann Robbins in Pontotoc, and her son George Shawhan in Baton Rouge. We are grateful to Leila Salisbury, Craig Gill, Emily Bandy, and others at the University Press of Mississippi for believing in this project.

A Note on the Author

Dorothy Sample Shawhan was born in Tupelo, Mississippi, in 1942 and came full circle when she died there in 2014. A life full in every way, a life rich and engaged. She was an outstanding educator and writer with degrees from Mississippi University for Women, Louisiana State University, and George Mason University. She kept a close association with the "W" and was undoubtedly aware of the outstanding student who preceded her there, Fannye Cook.

From 1970 to 1981, Shawhan worked as a writer and editor, first for publications at Indiana University in Bloomington, Indiana, and then for instructional television. In 1981, she moved to Cleveland, Mississippi, to teach at Delta State University, where she and I became colleagues and close friends. She served as chair of the Division of Languages and Literature from 1991 to 2006.

Shawhan's outstanding accomplishments as a teacher were recognized by a 2004 Mississippi Humanities Council Teacher Award. The many students Shawhan taught and mentored continue to sing her praises. One of her former students, Nathan Duff, paid tribute to her as a teacher in a column for the *Clarksdale Press Register*: "In her understated, thoughtful manner, she brought out the best in all of us."

Among her many recognitions are a Woman of Achievement award from the American Association of University Women, Alumna of the Year from Mississippi University for Women, the Mississippi Library Association's Fiction Writer of the Year, and the Lucy Howorth Award to outstanding women in the Delta, posthumously presented at Delta State University in 2015.

Passionate about conservation, she was a longtime board member and past president of Friends of Dahomey Wildlife National Refuge in Bolivar County, Mississippi. She was a lifelong active member of the Methodist Church and founding member of the Cleveland Habitat for Humanity. She served as board member and president of the Mississippi Institute of Arts and Letters, as board member of the University Press of Mississippi, and as an active member and president of the American Association of University Women.

Shawhan was alert to women who had been overlooked or underappreciated, and she devoted much of her career to writing about them and their contributions. Her first book, *Lizzie*, a novel published in 1995, was based on the life of Minnie Brewer, daughter of a Mississippi governor, who ran a feminist newspaper in Clarksdale, Mississippi, in the 1930s. In 2006 Shawhan coauthored with Martha Swain a biography of Lucy Somerville Howorth, or "Judge Lucy," from Cleveland, Mississippi, who was elected to the US House of Representatives in 1931. In 2011, Shawhan published a book on self-taught Cleveland artist Carolyn Norris, *Spirit of the Delta*. In 2012, she published an electronic version of *Going to Graceland*, a collection of short stories in the vein of Chaucer about a group of "pilgrims" journeying from New Orleans to Memphis to visit Elvis Presley's shrine at Graceland. A huge fan of Presley, her fellow Tupelo native, she wrote several stories about him. When she died, Shawhan had nearly completed her fifth book, *Fannye Cook: Mississippi's Passionate Conservationist.*

Dorothy was a storyteller. She could remember and retell countless family stories, not only her own. Her stories, both told and written, reflect her love for family and friends. Her published stories are filled with colorful characters, and even when rascals get their due, they're depicted with good-natured humor and compassion.

For *Tapestry*, a faculty literary journal she and I cofounded at Delta State, Dorothy wrote about biking in Amish country, counting loons in Maine, and losing her luggage in Paris on her way to Spain. Her stories set in the Mississippi Delta show a deep knowledge of the land and its inhabitants' sometimes irrational behavior over property. Her love for her Mississippi home, whether Tupelo or the Mississippi Delta, seeps through. For Dorothy, as for her namesake, there was no place like it.

Dorothy's accomplishments, outstanding as they are, can only suggest her spirit. Being with Dorothy meant laughing a lot. She had a wonderful laugh. She found humor in the most unlikely situations, and if things weren't funny, she'd make a wry comment—memorable, priceless—that got right to the heart of things. To my knowledge, she never got in a hurry and never said no to an invitation.

In her memorial remarks after the death of Judge Howorth, Dorothy recalled the words of Lucy's sister on hearing the news: "The world seems awfully empty." Those words came back to me when Dorothy died.

This book is Dorothy's tribute to Fannye Cook for her outstanding contributions to conservation and for enriching the lives of all who knew her. In reading Dorothy's words, you may also find that her own great spirit hovers nearby.

—Marion Barnwell

FANNYE COOK

ONE

Girlhood in Crystal Springs, 1889–1907

She lived with wild things.
—Rita Brignac Bizzell

When the wood thrushes arrived on the Mississippi Gulf Coast from their long southern migration, Fannye Cook would row out into the water, let the exhausted birds land on her and her boat, and row them back to shore.[1] Such action was characteristic of Fannye Cook, who had a passion for nature and all its creatures, and who devoted her life to their preservation in her home state. She worked for a strong conservation bill for six years at her own expense, she was a meticulous scientist and wrote books and articles on the plants and animals she collected, and she corresponded with some of the best minds in the country on the subject of science and conservation: Paul Bartsch and Alexander Wetmore of the Smithsonian Institution, Roger Conant of the Philadelphia Zoological Garden, Aldo Leopold, father of game management and co-founder of the Wilderness Society, and many others. In addition, her work was key in establishing the Mississippi Museum of Natural Science. All this she accomplished in an era when women had only recently been allowed to vote.

Born July 19, 1889, in Crystal Springs, Mississippi, the seventh of ten children, Frances Addine Cook was named for a great aunt. This aunt was also called Fanny, but her namesake would write her name with an *e*. Her parents, Gilbert Morris Cook and Martha Ellen Pierce, started their life together in rural Copiah County. G. M. Cook apparently shared his daughter's keen interest in the natural world. He told her how in 1878 passenger pigeons were still plentiful in the Pearl River swamp and that when his father was a child the flocks were "so large and so low that Daddy and other

Cook family portrait in the late nineteenth century.

school kids would run thru them with arms spread. The birds moved out of their way just far enough to keep from getting caught by the children."[2] In 1813 John James Audubon, riding on horseback from Louisville, Kentucky, to Henderson, Kentucky, witnessed this: "The air was literally filled with Pigeons. The light of noonday was obscured as by an eclipse, the dung fell in spots, not unlike melting flakes of snow; and the continued buzz of the wings had a tendency to lull my senses to repose."[3] In 1914, Martha, the last passenger pigeon known on earth, died in captivity in the Cincinnati Zoological Gardens. She was preserved through taxidermy and was to be shown through October 2015 at the Smithsonian Museum of Natural History as part of the exhibition "Once There Were Billions."[4] Audubon and generations of Cooks would be sorry to know this.

Gilbert Cook was born 1848 in Utica, Mississippi. His father died when he was only five years old, and he was sent out to work and live with different friends and relatives at the age of ten. One of his jobs was hauling logs for the building of Crystal Springs' Old Head House, which was used as a hospital for the wounded during the siege of Vicksburg.[5] Later he lived with his sister in Crystal Springs and went to school there. Unlike many teenagers, he was not lured by the siren call of the Civil War. At the age of twenty-one he traveled to the Texas panhandle with a relative and worked in the cotton fields. When he returned to Mississippi "riding a Texas pony," he continued to farm, and in 1873 married Martha Pierce. Gilbert rented land for about a year and then bought his own.

By 1902 the couple had ten children and had bought property in Crystal Springs. In 1911 they built the large house that still stands and that remained the house that Fannye would call "home" the rest of her life, regardless of where she lived.[6] Fannye's father apparently bequeathed to his daughter determination and perseverance—or phrased differently, stubbornness. One family member remembered that when anybody wanted to reference "real stubbornness" they would say, "Stubborn as G. M. Cook."[7]

Fannye Cook's mother, Martha Pierce, was clearly a strong person as well, though she was not as well documented as her husband. She was ten years younger than Gilbert and died nine years earlier than he; she gave birth to and raised seven girls and three boys, all of whom were respected, solid citizens. Linnie Jewel taught school and later worked for the Internal Revenue Service; William Daniel was a banker; Lucy Earl was a station agent for the Illinois Central Railroad; Alethia Belle was a farmer; Gilbert Pierce was an automobile dealer; Lena Mae lived in Panama with her engineer husband and was mother to Rita Bizzell; Frances (Fannye) Addine was the seventh child; Vivian Electra worked for the Welfare Department; Lewis Holloman was a farmer; and the baby, Launo Pearl, lived to be 102.[8]

Crystal Springs, as the name implies, was a serendipitous spot for Fannye Cook to get her start. Copiah County was once home to the Choctaws, as evidenced by arrow heads, mounds, pottery, jewelry, and skeletons. The county took its name from a particular band, the Koi-piah-bok, who lived on and reverenced the land before the Treaty of Doak's Stand in 1820.[9] Old Crystal Springs was founded about the same year by Methodist preacher Elisha Lott, who had herds of sheep and cattle and who was drawn there by the "rich soil, splendid woodland, abundant game, tall grasses, and canebrakes."[10] He was also drawn to the "bubbling fresh, pure water" of the springs.[11] Ironically, he brought his slaves with him but "was interested in ministering to the spiritual needs of the Choctaws."[12] Lott established a Methodist church there in 1826 that flourished over the next hundred years, operating a camp meeting beginning in the 1840s:[13] "people flocked to it for fifty miles and more in wagons and on horseback"[14] to attend the camp meetings and listen to the preaching.

The move from the old Crystal Springs three miles west to the Crystal Springs of today came with the railroad in 1858. Though many were skeptical, the citizens ultimately decided that their town should be on the tracks. The Methodists thought their church should be there too and built a white

Cook family home built in 1911 in Crystal Springs, Mississippi.

frame church with a "simple steeple."[15] This connection to the wider world brought great changes. The little Methodist church hosted the annual conference of the state's preachers in 1864, 1870, 1882, and 1889,[16] the year of Fannye's birth. She would attend church and Sunday school there in years to come.

The town's move to the railroad not only brought people in but took them and the fruits of their labors out as well. A local historian reported that "on one Tuesday, November 8, 1907, its people bought three hundred tickets to Jackson!" Fannye Cook, with her penchant for travel, could well have been among them. The historian further reports that "by 1919, its shipping was growing rapidly; and in that year Crystal Springs shipped 1350 cars of vegetables valued at a million and a half dollars!"[17] The tomato became the vegetable (or fruit, to be technical) of choice in Crystal Springs with Fannye's father among those planting and harvesting.[18] The town declared itself "Tomatopolis of the World" and held Tomato Festivals with parades, bands, speeches, and a Tomato Queen.[19]

The camp meetings that had begun in old Crystal Springs continued and grew with a tabernacle that seated four thousand and a few permanent cottages. These continued through forty-seven sessions until the beginning of World War I.[20] Crystal Springs also became home to the Mississippi Chautauqua Assembly from 1892 to 1917. One of its catalogues described it as having "the attracting charm of the circus; the wit and wisdom of the stage; the religious zeal of the pulpit; and the outdoor benediction of health, rest, and fellowship."[21] The assembly met on a lake surrounded by trees and paths for strolling. By 1916 there were eighty-eight cottages surrounding an amphitheater as well as a hotel and restaurant. People came by train from all over the South to socialize, swim, and boat, and to attend band concerts, lectures, and sermons.[22]

Crystal Springs also produced several prominent politicians. Joseph Weldon Bailey, born there in 1863, eventually became a US senator representing Texas. Bailey shared ancestry with Ellen Sullivan Woodward (1887–1971) from Louisville, Mississippi, who became director of the Women's and Professional Division of the WPA, and who was considered to be Roosevelt's second most powerful appointee after labor secretary Frances Perkins. Pat Harrison was born in Crystal Springs eight years before Fannye Cook. He graduated from public school as valedictorian in 1899, played semiprofessional baseball in the Old Tomato League, taught school, became a principal, studied law at night, and was admitted to the bar in 1902. He was elected to the US House of Representatives in 1911 and entered the Senate in 1919. Altogether he spent thirty years representing Mississippi in the legislature and, along with Woodward, was key in placing Mississippians to head up the Depression-era WPA projects, one of which would play an important part in Fannye Cook's career.

These Crystal Springs currents—gifts of nature, a sense of adventure, intellectualism, political savvy, and Methodism, with its emphasis on social consciousness—converged into a fertile stream for the launching of the young conservationist. Fannye Cook's large, lively family also offered opportunities to grow and learn. She was seventh in the birth order, and because the three brothers reportedly "looked after" the sisters,[23] Fannye would take as her mission to look after the natural world. When asked if Fannye had pets, her niece replied, "She lived with wild things."[24] Reportedly even in childhood, Fannye began collecting "specimens of Mississippi wild plants, birds, mammals, and amphibians."[25]

Cook sisters in early 1900s. Above, left to right: Belle, Lucy Earl, Lena Mae; below, left to right: Vivian, Jewel, Launo, Fannye.

Cook family reunion, 1950. Fannye in top row in polka dot dress.

One is reminded of Charles Darwin's life in the previous century. An avid collector with a quest to understand the processes of nature, he may well have inspired Cook. Darwin's preoccupation with the natural world and his collection of finches in the Galapagos Islands led him to his theory of natural selection.[26] He lived with his wife and ten children in Down House south of London and wrote his *On the Origin of Species* there in 1859. Assisted by his children, he carried out many experiments there with carnivorous plants, bees, barnacles, and earthworms. He had a particular obsession with earthworms, those tillers of the earth, and said, "It may be doubted whether there are many other animals which have played so important a part in the history of the world as have these lowly organized creatures."[27] Fannye's main interest was birds at this stage, but she undoubtedly contemplated the earthworm as part of their diet and later would contemplate it for itself.

President Theodore Roosevelt in Mississippi and Beyond

In 1902, when Fannye was thirteen years old, Teddy Roosevelt came to Mississippi. As a child, Roosevelt was fascinated with nature and, like Fannye Cook, collected and preserved mice, birds, and salamanders. He had seriously considered a career in science before he was caught up in public life.[28]

He came to Mississippi, to Sharkey County, not far from the Cooks' Copiah County, on a hunting trip. The expedition was led by Holt Collier, a former slave and a well-known bear hunter said to have killed over three thousand bears in his lifetime. Among the hunting party were journalists and well-known big game hunters such as John Avery McIlhenny of Avery Island, Louisiana, who had served with Roosevelt in the Rough Riders during the Spanish-American War.

Collier and his dogs tracked a large male bear and bugled for Roosevelt and party to come quickly. But when the bear killed one of Collier's dogs, Collier whacked the bear over the head, lassoed him, and tied him to a tree. When Roosevelt arrived on the scene, he refused to shoot the bloody bear, though another in the party killed him with a knife. Subsequently the *Washington Post* published Clifford Berryman's cartoon "Drawing the Line in Mississippi." The cartoon depicts the president refusing to shoot a little bear cub. Then the American entrepreneurial spirit took over, and the teddy bear was born.

Collier served Roosevelt on another bear hunt in Louisiana in 1907. Collier died in 1936 and is buried in Greenville. Named in his honor is the Holt Collier National Wildlife Refuge.[29] In 1943, Cook would write in *The Game Animals of Mississippi* that bears could still be found in Hooker's Ridge not far from the site of the president's hunt.

The next year the president went on his famous camping trip in the Sierras with naturalist John Muir, a trip that launched the national conservationist movement, if not the one in Mississippi. Mississippi's conservation launch would wait several more years for Fannye Cook, who had to get through school first.

Crystal Springs' first public school was the Peabody Institute (1869–75), held in what had been a private home and would later be a boarding house and hotel. Linnie Jewel, the first born of Fannye's siblings, was a student there.[30] When Fannye was two years old, Crystal Springs built a new graded public school, a two-story frame building with a bell tower. The school started with only a few students, but by the time Fannye was in high school, enrollment had grown to over four hundred students. She attended during the school years 1903–5.[31] The faculty was said to be superior. The education was not completely free, however. To help pay for coal to stoke the iron stoves throughout the building and for chalk and erasers, students were charged fifty cents per month. If they didn't pay, students were not graded.[32]

TWO

Columbus to College, 1907–11

Her song was only living aloud
Her work, a singing with her hand.
—Sidney Lanier

After high school, Fannye flew the nest 120 miles northeast to Columbus, Mississippi, to enroll in the Industrial Institute and College (II&C). She was eighteen years old. The average cost of board was twelve dollars a month and tuition was free for five years.[1] II&C had been established in 1884, six years before Fannye Cook's birth, "for white girls" by the Mississippi legislature and was the first state college in the nation founded for women. It would later be called Mississippi State College for Women and still later Mississippi University for Women. The founders envisioned it as a place where the daughters of poor white farming families could be educated and thereby better themselves.[2]

When Fannye enrolled, various courses of study were offered. The Normal course was for those young women who wanted to teach in the state's public schools. The College course offered "literary and scientific training" with the bachelor of arts and bachelor of science degrees. Industrial courses (including bookkeeping, stenography, dressmaking, millinery, and home science) and music courses were also available. Physical education was required of all students at the instigation of president Henry Lewis Whitfield and the innovative physical education instructor Miss Emma Ody Pohl.[3] Fannye's tenure at the women's college coincided with many of the early faculty and administrators whose names mark buildings on the Mississippi University for Women campus—Whitfield, Orr, Fant, Peyton, Keirn, Poindexter, and Shattuck.[4]

Having grown up with six sisters, Fannye probably adapted easily to dormitory life. The uniforms must have been a burden, though, for one more comfortable with wild things. The navy blue gored skirt reached to the floor and the untrimmed navy blue blouse had long sleeves.[5] Fannye completed both the Normal course, which qualified her to teach, and the bachelor of arts in English and History. In addition to the usual academic courses, the Normal curriculum included Sight Singing, Drawing-Manual Training, Agriculture, and Practice School.[6] President Whitfield, a progressive agrarian, was a strong advocate for the study of agriculture and horticulture for young women and encouraged the classes to grow gardens when Fannye was a student there. In fact, his attempt to establish a demonstration farm for the college would later lead to his abrupt dismissal by the board of trustees.[7]

More successful toward Whitfield's goal of improved health for Mississippians was his hiring of Emma Ody Pohl, the energetic young teacher from Greenville. She joined the faculty in 1907, organized the department, and began to teach dance classes and to develop ceremonies such as the May Day pageant and the Zouave drill based on French military routines. These would become part of the college's rich traditions.[8] State examinations for license to teach included the subjects of "Algebra, Geometry, Caesar, Virgil, Latin Grammar and Composition, Rhetoric, English Literature, Theory and Practice of Teaching, General History, Civil Government, and either Greek, Chemistry, or Physical Geography, and Physics."[9] If a student in the Normal wanted a bachelor's degree as well, she could take thirty-two hours in the junior and senior years.[10]

To earn the AB in English and History, Fannye would have come under the influence of Miss Pauline Orr, professor of English language and literature, one of the original II&C faculty members. Student Emma May Laney remembers Miss Orr's "zest" that went beyond the classroom. She remembers "one hot afternoon in April when a class of twenty-five followed her in a long blue line (we went outside the gates in those days only with a chaperone) on a dusty walk of five miles to see wild Hawthorne in bloom—all because we had heard her read Browning's 'Oh, to be in England now that April's there.'"[11] Miss Orr would later resign in protest when President Whitfield eliminated Latin and modern language from the requirements for a BS in home economics. She became a full-time suffragette and moved to New York City.[12]

President William Howard Taft visited the II&C campus in 1909. He was touring the South and made a stop in Columbus because his secretary of war, J. M. Dickerson, was from Lowndes County.[13] Taft ate possum and marched "a path strewn with rose petals" to Music Hall where he talked about educating women: "A girl has the right to demand such training that she can win her own way to independence, thereby making marriage not a necessity, but a choice."[14]

Marriage nonetheless worked its way into many of the college's traditions, if not into Fannye's head. A Gingko tree had been set out on campus in 1900 as part of an experiment by the Department of Agriculture,[15] and a Gingko grew on the Mississippi Agricultural and Mechanical (A&M) College campus as well. The legend grew that if a boy stood under the tree at the men's college and a girl under the tree at the women's college and a leaf fell on each of their heads, they were destined to marry. Fannye, with her realistic bent, would have dismissed such fancies.

Fannye's sister Vivian, two years younger than she, joined her at II&C after she graduated from high school. She took the Industrial and the Normal routes, courses that would assure her of a job. And in the future she would often work with Fannye on projects such as the Plant and Animal Survey of the WPA.

Many of the young women who were II&C students during Fannye's years there furthered their educations and achieved prominence in their fields. Elizabeth Lee Hazen went on to become the first woman to earn a doctorate in biomedicine from Columbia and is known for isolating the antibiotic nystatin.[16] Helen C. Carloss became a lawyer and served on a US court of appeals; Frances Jones Gaither became a best-selling novelist.[17] Clytee Evans graduated in 1911 and returned with a doctorate to teach biology there for forty years. She would tell Mississippi State College for Women Alumnae secretary Marcie Sanders in 1980 that Fannye Cook "was the most talented alumna in the history of the institution in her opinion."[18]

When Fannye received the Normal Diploma, she left II&C for the school year 1908–9 to teach all grades in West, Mississippi, for a salary of fifty-eight dollars per month. She left West to "return to college."[19] Perhaps she left II&C to teach because she needed the money; or perhaps teaching all grades convinced her to return for the AB degree.

Fannye Cook's profile picture in the 1911–12 *Meh Lady*, the college's yearbook, resembles a young Virginia Woolf, her dark hair parted in the middle

Fannye Cook.....Crystal Springs, Miss.

"Her song was only living aloud,
Her work, a singing with her hand."

Fannye, upon meeting a friend, relaxes thoroughly; her face glows with an enchanted smile. Some may think that she, ever ready to comfort and console others, has no troubles of her own. But to those who know her best she speaks of her aspirations hindered by trials. Fannye, however, knows not the meaning of failure, for to her failures are merely incentives to more earnest strivings. Should the fates of destiny be prevailed uopn to reveal her future, you would behold one of the State's most brilliant women scattering seeds of kindness and training the youth to a brighter, fuller appreciation of life.

Chairman of the Social Service Committee, Normal Diploma, and A.B. degree.

Cook in the 1911–12 *Meh Lady*, Industrial Institute and College yearbook.

and pulled back in a bun, a white lace dress. The quotation accompanying the picture is "Her song was only living aloud, / Her work, a singing with her hand." The lines come from a poem, "Life and Song," by Sidney Lanier. The poet expresses the wish that his art and his life be fused as one, but he, of course, uses the masculine pronoun: "His song was only living aloud, / His work, a singing with his hand."

Since Fannye was an English major, perhaps the yearbook editors were envisioning her as a writer, but the lines from Lanier as well as the paragraph accompanying her picture could be considered prophetic. A further description is offered:

> Fannye, upon meeting a friend, relaxes thoroughly; her face glows with an enchanted smile. Some may think, that she, ever ready to comfort and console others, has no troubles of her own. But to those who knew her best she speaks of her aspirations hindered by trials. Fannye, however, knows not the meaning of failure, for to her failures are merely incentives to more earnest strivings. Should the fates of destiny be prevailed upon to reveal her future, you would behold one of the State's most brilliant women scattering seeds of kindness and training the youth to a brighter, fuller appreciation of life.
>
> Chairman of the Social Service Committee,
> Normal Diploma, and A.B. degree[20]

Did Fannye Cook, even then, dream of being a force in conserving her state's natural resources and of educating the young to do likewise? Were her trials economic? Did she know her path would be easier were she a man? We can only speculate.

THREE

School Principal, Teacher, and Student, 1911–18

You couldn't be around her without learning something.
—Rita Brignac Bizzell

In the years after Fannye Cook's graduation from II&C, we see a young woman searching for her niche in a world where women did not yet have the vote and where men dominated the world of science. Like Eudora Welty, she must have associated, whether consciously or unconsciously, independence with travel,[1] because she was a rolling stone during these years.

From 1911 to 1915, she served as principal and teacher in the towns of Beauregard, West Point, and Louisville, Mississippi. Fresh out of college, she put her abilities to good use close to home, but clearly she wanted more. For two months in the summer of 1913, she attended the University of Colorado to study English and history.[2] "You couldn't be around her without learning something," said her niece Rita Brignac Bizzell.[3] Cook's next stop would be the Panama Canal and life for a time with her sister Lena Mae's family.

Lena Mae Cook, the sister just above Fannye in the birth order, had fallen in love with George DeMas Brignac, originally from the French settlement in Louisiana. Jewell, the oldest of the Cook siblings, had taught Brignac, and he had thus met Lena Mae. Once again Theodore Roosevelt's actions were of interest to the Cooks when he acquired rights to build the Panama Canal. George Brignac was employed in the building of the Canal, and, Lena Mae's father, Gilbert Cook, took her to Panama by boat to marry him in August of 1913.[4]

When she was twenty-six years old, Fannye Cook applied to teach in the Panama Canal Zone and listed as her present address Cristobal, Panama. In the application, she describes herself as being 5 feet 8½ inches tall and weighing 133 pounds. She writes that she is only fluent in English but can teach Latin and German, and that she prefers teaching tenth grade, with fourth grade her second choice. W. H. Smith had been her employer when she left II&C for a year to teach and in 1915 he was Mississippi state superintendent of education and writes Cook an extremely positive reference with no weak points noted. He considers her strongest points to be "in discipline and in instruction."[5]

The US government opened its first public school in Panama in January of 1906.[6] The schools were racially segregated. The white schools served the children of workers and of US military personnel.[7] The black schools were made up predominantly of workers recruited from the West Indies, with a few black US citizens.[8] The high school building in Cristobal is described as "an outstanding school plant" and is pictured as a multi-winged structure of Spanish design with a tower, arched windows, and palm trees.[9] English and history were required subjects, which would have been in Fannye Cook's favor, as well as her teaching experience. That she lived with the Brignacs would have also helped her secure employment since it was extremely difficult for single women to find suitable accommodations and most who taught there lived with friends or family.[10]

Fannye Cook was hired to teach in the Cristobal High School beginning in the fall of 1915 with a salary of ninety dollars per month. In November she became ill and missed twelve days of school, but returned to finish out the school year. On her "Efficiency Report" she received "Excellent" in all categories except "General Workmanship," where she was rated "Very Good." There was "No Report" on her "Executive or supervisory ability." She returned to the United States for the summer of 1916 and is listed as a passenger on the SS *Cartago*, which arrived in New Orleans on July 7, 1916, from Cristobal, Canal Zone.[11] She returned to Panama and taught in Cristobal a second year through June 1917.[12]

Fannye Cook's niece Rita was born to the Brignacs on April 30, 1917. Rita was greatly influenced by her aunt, and they would form a close personal and professional attachment in the coming years. Rita majored in the sciences, and would later assist her aunt with the WPA Mississippi Plant and Animal Survey.

When the assassination of Archduke Ferdinand in Sarajevo triggered World War I in June of 1914, the war must have seemed far away from Mississippi and from Panama, but when the United States joined the conflict on the side of the Allied Powers in 1917, the women of Crystal Springs began to knit socks for the soldiers.[13] One of Fannye Cook's contemporaries, Minnie Brewer, daughter of Earl Brewer, Mississippi governor from 1912 to 1916, exaggerated her age and volunteered to watch for enemy ships along the Jersey Shore.[14] In Louisville, Mississippi, Ellen Woodward helped organize a chapter of the Red Cross.[15] Mississippian Lucy Somerville worked in a munitions factory in New York City.[16] Fannye Cook would have still been in Panama in June of 1917 when General Pershing landed in France and saw the Americans' first action at Chateau-Thierry. What impact might that news have had on her?

Apparently Fannye Cook decided to go west. She took a job in Lander, Wyoming, as high school principal for the 1917–18 school year. Her annual salary was $810.[17] Nothing is known about what drew her to Wyoming or who, but her leaving was noted in the *Wyoming State Journal:* "Miss Fannye Cook, who was principal of the Lander High School in 1917, is now engaged in war work in Washington, D.C. at a salary of $2,500 a year."[18] One glimpse of her in the West comes from Eudora Welty, who came to know Cook very well in the years she boarded in the Welty home. Welty writes, "Once in the West she was climbing a mountain and as she got level with the top she saw a rattlesnake looking right into her eyes. She just looked right back. She knew all about him."[19]

Cook was possibly drawn to Washington by the promise of a better salary (though the Lander report was inflated), by a desire to participate in the war effort, and by family ties. Here she would hone her political skills and continue to develop her passion for the wild things.

FOUR

The Washington Years, 1918–26

> If you don't take care of yourself you will never be account in your old days quit going so much and sleep more. Well good-bye, your devoted
> Mother

A letter to Fannye Cook from the Treasury Department dated November 14, 1918, informs her that she has been appointed a clerk in the Office of the Commissioner of Internal Revenue for a salary of $1200 per annum. Three days earlier Germany had surrendered, bringing World War I to a close. Cook took the oath of office before a notary public on November 22, and her "Personal History" filed that day lists a sister in the War Department, a sister in the Post Office Department, and a brother-in-law in the Mechanical Department. These were Linnie Jewell, Vivian, and George Brignac.[1] Perhaps Senator Pat Harrison, with whom the Cook family shared Crystal Springs as hometown, was instrumental in acquiring these jobs.[2]

While there is no evidence that Fannye Cook was directly involved in the suffrage movement, she was surely aware of the struggle unfolding in Washington to gain the vote for women. And given what we know of her life, she must surely have believed that women should have full citizenship. When Cook arrived in Washington, members of Alice Paul's Woman's Party and of Carrie Chapman Catt and Maud Wood Park's National American Woman Suffrage Association (NAWSA) were in the final years of the long battle for the vote. Marches and arrests of women picketers were the order of the day.[3] Cook's fellow Mississippian and devout Methodist Nellie Nugent Somerville, mother of Lucy Somerville Howorth, had served as vice president of the NAWSA. In 1923 Somerville would become the first woman to be elected to the Mississippi legislature.[4]

The Nineteenth Amendment, granting women the vote, had been drafted and introduced in 1878 by Susan B. Anthony and Elizabeth Cady Stanton. Finally it was passed by Congress in 1919 and sent out for the requisite number of states to ratify. On August 18, 1920, the southern state of Tennessee voted for ratification and thus votes for women became law. Fannye Cook and her sisters must have felt gratified by this development and would have been on hand for celebrations in the nation's capital. Their home state would not ratify the Nineteenth Amendment until 1984.

The IRS seems a vast distance from what would be Cook's life work, but its reputation was a bit different in those days than it has become today. The agency helped put away racketeers and finance World War I and was in general not eyed with as much suspicion as has become its fate.[5] Cook's job was to audit individual tax returns, and she must have been good at it. She was promoted each year of her IRS employment, being reappointed in 1924 for $2300 per annum.[6]

Correspondence

Correspondence from Fannye Cook's family back home in Crystal Springs gives a human side to her frequent moves in Washington. A letter from her mother in 1919 indicates that Fannye, Linnie Jewell, and Vivian were together at 39 Q Street in Washington, DC, that Fannye had been in the hospital, and that her mother hopes "she will soon be strong." She gives no indication of what Fannye's illness was. She writes of quilting, dress patterns, and other domestic issues, and then closes with advice:

> If you don't take care of yourself you will never be any account in your old days quit going so much and sleep more. Well good-bye, your devoted
>
> Mother[7]

A letter from their father to his "dear girls" was addressed to 104 Woodley Apts., Washington, DC. He tells them that the local Baptist preacher is coming to Washington for his convention and will probably call on them. He thinks the preacher is "a right fine fellow but he is a Baptist."

By 1922, correspondence indicates that Fannye was living at 1319 N Street NW. She would not get home for Christmas, but a letter from "Sis" (probably

Vivian) thanks her for her card to their mother and fills her in on some local happenings: "Cuz Will Frances had a fight last Sunday a.m. and is badly *blued* on the face. He came by and brought us a mess of spareribs and of sausage today." A letter to Jewell and Fannye from their father and dated 1922–23 says that they have sent them a large fruit cake by parcel post. He expresses thanks to the Lord for their good children. He says that the "cold whistle" has blown four times, and he is worried about the young cabbage plants. He says that their mother has been trying to "pay up some of her visiting debts," and judging from the list of names that follows, she was quite a sociable woman.

In a November 1923 letter to Fannye, her father begins by apologizing for not answering every letter she writes to them and assures her that they love her. "If you live to have as many dear children scattered over the country as we do, you will understand better why letters are so far apart."

The IRS notwithstanding, Fannye had evidently not forgotten her passion, because she enrolled in the Columbian College of Arts and Sciences at George Washington University in the study of ornithology in 1923[8] and came under the influence of Dr. Paul Bartsch, who had begun scientific and systematic bird banding in North America in 1902. He banded twenty-three Black-crowned Night Herons in the District of Columbia. The bands were serially numbered and had the address to which they should be returned. The first was returned in September 1902, and Bartsch published the result in 1904. He writes:

> There are still many unsolved problems about bird life, among them are the age that birds attain, the exact time at which birds acquire their adult dress, and the changes which occur in this with years. Little, too, is known about the laws and routes of bird migration, and much less about the final disposition of the untold thousands which are annually produced.[9]

Dr. Alexander Wetmore was another distinguished ornithologist that Cook came to know at the Smithsonian. He was only three years older than Cook and, like Cook, had become interested in birds as a child. When he was five years old, his mother gave him Chapman's *Handbook of Birds in Eastern North America*. His first field entry was an observation of a pelican in Florida: "a great big bird that eats fish." After college he worked with the US Bureau of Biological Survey and in 1924 he joined the Smithsonian.[10]

These connections would be a major force in the advancement of Fannye Cook's life's work.

In April of 1924, her mother writes Fannye to thank her for the check. Though she's "crazy about roses," she's glad Fannye decided to send the check because she "sent Dad right back to town to get three flower pots," and she will "go to town this week and get a hat for Easter." This was followed by a long community report.

In September of 1924, Cook abruptly resigned from the IRS because of "gross discrimination on the part of the Chief of Personal Audit Review Section and the Head of Personal Audit Division, Income Tax." A series of handwritten notes on her letter from various administrators indicates that Cook had expressed dissatisfaction with her grade. Her resignation was accepted "without prejudice" on October 6, 1924.[11]

This intriguing information raises all kinds of questions. Did she discover that men of the same rank were making more? Did she find that more flirtatious women were making more? Was she passed over for promotion in favor of someone with a lesser record for efficiency? In what ways had her superior exhibited "gross discrimination"? Whatever the reason, the resignation did not bring her back to Mississippi immediately. Her connections to George Washington University and to the Smithsonian kept her in the District of Columbia awhile longer.

A 1924 Christmas season letter to Fannye from Jewell in Crystal Springs says that she doesn't know if she'll go back to Washington or not. Her job there is uncertain, their parents are not well, and she says, "It is hard for them to be alone." They all wish Fannye could be home for Christmas, "but you are here in the summer" and they "couldn't expect you now."

Perhaps this letter did bring Fannye home, because collection records indicate that in November and December of that year, she collected skins of the Green-winged Teal, Northern Flicker, Eastern Bluebird, Loggerhead Shrike, Red-winged Blackbird, Winter Wren, Red-tailed Hawk, Ring-necked Duck, Mallard, Eastern Towhee, Savannah Sparrow, Pileated Woodpecker, and Black Vulture. The collections were made in Bolivar, Copiah, and Warren Counties, and she was apparently a very good shot. Her bird collections continue into 1925 with some forty specimens added from a number of Delta counties as well as Harrison on the Gulf coast. The months cited for the collections indicate that she was home in Crystal Springs a great deal during this year.[12]

Records from the Smithsonian National Museum of Natural History show that many of the Mississippi collections made their way back to Washington with Fannye. Birds, mammals, plants, reptiles, mollusks, and even fossils Cook collected around Mississippi are now part of the national collections.[13] Whether she realized it at this point or not, she was honing her skills in taxidermy and plant preservation to bring back home.

Before Thanksgiving Day in November 1925, Gilbert Cook writes Fannye in Washington. He begins by teasing her that his horse had aged greatly since taking her to the train, and he looks like he's had a great scare. Then he goes to say, "I am sure you did the best your gender would let you." He and Martha have had a "happy time since the anniversary" (their forty-second) and "our hearts often overflow with joy when in the calm moments of the day when gratitude to our children takes possession of our whole being for their expressions of love for us." Thanksgiving will be spent with Lucy Earl, he writes, and he promises to send a *Meteor* for the local news—"saves writing, ha, ha." Their mother is writing Jewel (who apparently decided to go back to Washington) and so he won't write her, but asks Fannye to let her read this letter. He ends by saying, "So with a bushel of love for each of you, I am ever your Dad G.M.Cook."

The biological collections catalog at the Mississippi Museum of Natural Science cites very few collections in 1926, probably because Fannye had become political. A letter to Jewell from her father on March 22, 1926, says that he guesses "Fannie is very much disappointed, W.D., not being able to get the bill passed by the Senate that she was so much interested in well such is life, we are awful sorry but can't be helped." (The reference is to Fannye's brother William Daniel Cook, who was in the legislature at that time.) Another on March 30, 1926, says that he did the best he knew how with her bulletins and that he hopes "you can get such information as you deserve; hello here comes your mother with another arm full" of bulletins, and also a book. He writes that means they will have to add another sheet. Apparently Fannye Cook's campaign for conservation in Mississippi had begun from the nation's capital with her own family on the front line.

House Bill No. 329, an amendment to a weak 1922 law, did pass the Mississippi legislature on March 19, 1926, but it was not one that pleased Fannye Cook. The board of supervisors of each county could appoint a bird, game, and fish warden who held office for two years and could have as many deputies as he wanted. Hunting seasons with hunting licenses, game limits, and restrictions on certain guns were to be enforced, but were not likely to be in counties where everybody knew each other. The bill provided for no central state oversight body.[14]

The Washington years were extremely important in Cook's development. Though her day job was auditing tax returns, her passion led her to graduate study in ornithology, where she completed all but the thesis. She forged valuable contacts with scientists at the Smithsonian and the Bureau of Biological Survey.[15] Dr. Paul Bartsch would become her correspondent and mentor. But in 1926 she was ready to take her fight to establish a wildlife commission to the home front.

FIVE

Bringing the Fight Home, 1926–32

The bird's-eye view you [Aldo Leopold] gave me
of your plans for future work was inspirational.
—Fannye Cook

John Muir is considered the father of America's conservation movement. He migrated from Scotland in 1849 when he was a boy and later worked in a carriage factory in Indianapolis. He lost his sight as a result of an accident at the factory, and as he tried to recover in a darkened room, friends came and read to him about wildernesses like Yosemite. Muir promised himself that if he got his sight back, he would give up machinery and study the wild. His sight did return, and in 1867 he set off on a thousand-mile hike from Kentucky to Cedar Keys, Florida, "going by the wildest, leafiest and least trodden way I could find." The records of the journey would later be published in *A Thousand-Mile Walk to the Gulf*. From there he took a boat to Cuba and went on to New York and then California, where he would work for the precursor of the coast guard. He would go on to found the Sierra Club, and in 1903 he would go on his famous camping trip in the back country of Yosemite with President Roosevelt, the genesis of our national park system.[1]

Muir said the forests of America "must have been a great delight to God, for they were the best he ever planted. . . . About five hundred species of trees . . . —lordly monarchs proclaiming the gospel of beauty like apostles."[2] The clear-cutting of the forests of Mississippi was one of the factors that led Fannye Cook, surely Mississippi's mother of conservation, to come back to her own state in 1926 and to begin her campaign with the evangelical zeal of Muir. David Watts and William Turcotte describe the Mississippi scene like this:

> By 1900, Mississippi was a leading timber exporting state. The "cut out and get out" policy adopted by many loggers left millions of acres here bare and subject to erosion, later to be further degraded by wildfire and uncontrolled grazing practices. Lumber operators had little regard for wildlife, and loggers and market hunters systematically killed off forest game. The forest resources that had covered 95 percent of the state in 1800 were practically gone by 1930.[3]

Market hunting was the practice of wholesale killing of edible or fur-bearing wildlife to sell and ship away for consumption in other states and was a factor that helped forge the bond between conservationists and Mississippi's hunters.

Mary Hamilton, in her autobiography *Trials of the Earth*, has left us a remarkable inside look at the clear-cutting of Mississippi. Born in 1866, married to a mysterious Englishman at age eighteen, she moved with him to the logging camps in the virgin forests of the Delta.

Hamilton ran a boarding house for the loggers, cooked for 115 men, bore children, buried children, and in her old age was prompted by a young journalist, Helen Dick Davis, to write her life's story. She obliged and in 1933 gave Davis a manuscript of 150,000 words that she called "the true happenings of my life." The manuscript languished in a trunk until it was published in 1992 by the University Press of Mississippi. Hamilton's family subsequently became aware of the work and republished it in 2012. The original manuscript was donated to the Capps Archives at Delta State University. In her foreword to the 1992 edition of the work, Ellen Douglas writes:

> One of the delights of this book is Mary Hamilton's evocation of the natural world she lives in—of the power of the river and of the wild lonely forests, still resounding with panther screams and the howls of wolves. It seems almost a sin to paraphrase, when her own words serve so well. "We went from Gunnison [to Concordia Island] in a two-horse buggy," she writes. "Frank and Jim on horseback. We drove down the Mississippi River levee about a mile, then turned off the levee into the thickest timber I had ever seen. Oak, gum, ash, hackberry, and poplar wood so thick, with no underbrush, only big blue cane growing rank and tall,

> almost to the limbs of the trees. . . . When we came out on the Mississippi River, the ground was sandy, but it was black sand, and the woods were thinner, there were fewer trees but larger—big old cottonwoods and sycamores that seemed to me when I looked up like their tops were lost in the sky. . . . The soft black sand was almost hub deep."[4]

One can only imagine a meeting and conversation between Mary Hamilton and Fannye Cook, two women with vastly different experiences but with a strong connection in their feelings for the natural world.

Down in Louisiana, another of Cook's contemporaries, Caroline Dormon, was also a woman who appreciated and worked to conserve "the wild things."[5] In fact Cook and Dormon shared a birthday, July 19, though Dormon was born a year before Cook. Dormon, like Cook, taught school briefly before becoming a full-time naturalist. She was the first woman to be hired by the US Forestry Department and one of the first persons to promote a national forest in Louisiana. A talented artist, she painted the flora and fauna around her. Like Cook, she was always an educator. One of her titles with the Louisiana Forestry Division was "Supervisor, Forestry Education of the Department of Conservation."[6]

Fannye Cook began her Mississippi campaign in 1926 with the energy and zeal of a John Muir, a Caroline Dormon, or an evangelist. She traveled around the state largely at her own expense, making talks to clubs and parent-teacher associations (PTAs), staging exhibits at state fairs, enlisting people of all ages in her conservation cause, and continuing to collect birds, though the number of skins collected and identified declined as she mounted her campaign.

County fairs offered a good forum for Cook's poster displays, and after a fair in Laurel, she was asked to come to the Meridian fair. Her posters focused on how useful birds are in controlling harmful insects, and they caught the attention of Professor R. W. Harned of Mississippi A&M College, head of the State Plant Board, then most concerned with the insect problem. A huge boost to Cook's campaign came when Professor Harned offered her office space in the Biology Building at the A&M College, now Mississippi State University.[7]

She writes her mentor Dr. Bartsch on August 4, 1926, a long handwritten letter from Crystal Springs and says this about her new office space. "I've always had a decided dislike for basements. Don't see why it couldn't have been the attic, but you may be sure I haven't chirped. It is nice enough to get into the basement after sitting on the steps since January." She continues describing plans for her campaign that include raising money, lecturing with illustrations, and collecting. She asks if he knows of anyone who might have "moving pictures of wood creatures that might be had for use." She reminds Bartsch that she's left some of her bird "skins" there, as well as her wildflowers. Eminent professor Dr. Robert F. Griggs kiddingly called these her "hay." "I am thinking of having them sent to the University of Miss.," she says, "where from time to time I can name the various plants and pet them a little. Each specimen is worth a million dollars to me."

On the fourth page, she injects a firm note into this otherwise friendly, chatty letter. She reminds Bartsch that he failed to post credit for the work she did there last session. "Won't you be good enough to straighten this out right away. I paid full tuition both years and am entitled to full credit provided the work is satisfactory." She then returns to friendly letter mode, writing that her mother and father had been vacationing and that she has "tried her hand at housekeeping." She informs Bartsch that she has also visited her brother's plantation near Saint Joseph, Louisiana, from which she sent the distinguished ornithologist Dr. Alexander Wetmore "specimens of painted buntings" for which he had asked.[8] She sends regards to all Bartsch's colleagues and offers any help she could give from Mississippi. She ends with an inquiry:

> Tell me where I may find a collecting gun like yours. I think mine isn't sufficient and I remember yours is small and light as well as splendid. With my best wishes, I remain
>
> Sincerely yours,
> Fannye A. Cook.[9]

Ironically, while it was clear-cutting, fire, and drought in her home state that had brought her home, the next year Mississippi suffered the devastating 1927 flood that wreaked havoc in the Delta. Whereas previously Cook had collected in Bolivar and Sharkey counties, the few collections in 1927 were around Crystal Springs and Mississippi A&M College. She writes Dr. Bartsch that, two years before, she had collected specimens and made notes on wildlife in the area that is now under water. She wants to return to those flooded areas to follow up, hopes for funding from the American Legion, and asks Dr. Bartsch to write some letters in support.[10]

Four months later she writes Bartsch on Mississippi Association for the Conservation of Wild Life letterhead that the American Legion had decided their funds could be used only for relief work. The association, she explains, "grew out of my feeling keenly the need of a working force that could reach every nook and corner of the state before the legislature convenes in January." She summarizes her summer like this:

> During the summer I visited nine state normals, lecturing to thousands of teachers, conducted nature study classes and tours at three county 4H Club Camps, conducted a series of nature tours for the 4H Club Leadership Girls, lectured to large groups of farm women and to more than a thousand children who assembled at this Institution (A & M College) for a Club Congress. Have met in session with 10 county Boards of Supervisors to secure cooperation that would enable our new Association to do education work in behalf of conservation in the respective counties.[11]

At the end of this typewritten paragraph, Cook writes by hand, "all gratis."

She goes on to write that she "could weep over not having more time for field work but if one chooses to do pioneer work, he must be willing to blaze the trail." She says she is spending a great deal of time "in formulating [the] bill and in making it sufficiently popular to assure its passage."[12]

Passage of the bill to establish a wildlife commission was years away, but meanwhile Fannye Cook would continue to work tirelessly for its passage.

Mississippi Association for the Conservation of Wild Life Founded, 1927

Like her contemporary, Lucy Somerville (later Howorth), a young lawyer practicing in Cleveland, Mississippi, Cook believed forming organizations of like-minded people was the best way to accomplish goals for the common good. In that spirit she organized the Mississippi Association for the Conservation of Wild Life with herself as executive secretary. Among those she enlisted in the organization were early conservationists and leading Mississippi businessmen: R. W. Harned of Starkville, J. W. Tucker of Jackson, R. D. "Bob" Morrow, Ben M. Stevens of Richton, Judge W. E. McIntyre Sr. of Brandon, and W. G. McGill of New Albany.[13] The game laws on the books, passed in 1922 and 1926, provided for the sale of hunting licenses by the counties and the employment of game wardens, but the law did not have conservation as its focus. For an annual membership fee of one dollar, Cook promised Mississippi the following list:

- More sport for the sportsman
- More furs for the trapper
- More fish in the streams
- More beneficial hawks and owls to eat field rats and field mice
- More song birds in town and country
- More holly, wild crabapples, dogwood and azalea [*sic*] to beautify roadsides and woodlands.
- More boys and girls, men and women who love the outdoors and who go there with seeing eyes and hearing ears.[14]

The organization also supported creating wildlife refuges and a state department of conservation "to enforce the game laws, to investigate the economic status of our native fauna and flora, to establish and care for sanctuaries and shooting grounds and to educate the people in conservation, [with] all support [coming] from hunting licenses."[15] Mississippi was the only state that did not have such an agency.[16]

Cook's adversaries were market hunters and Mississippians who had always assumed they could hunt and fish almost anywhere, and certainly on their own land. Her supporters included the State Plant Board, the State Department of Education, the State Teachers Association, the American Legion, the Daughters of the American Revolution, PTAs, hunting and fishing clubs, the Mississippi Forestry Association, the Federation of Women's Clubs, the YWCA and Girl Reserves, and a variety of other civic groups.[17]

The goal of Cook's association was to spearhead the drive for a state law establishing a state wildlife commission. In 1928, the American Legion and state garden clubs backed this legislation.[18] The Speaker of the House of Representatives, Thomas L. Bailey, from the Delta, favored it too, but it failed to pass.[19] This setback must have been a grave disappointment to Fannye Cook.

Aldo Leopold in Mississippi, 1928

The man considered the foremost conservationist of the twentieth century, Aldo Leopold, traveled to Mississippi in 1928 to conduct a game survey under the sponsorship of the Game Restoration Committee of the Sporting Arms and Ammunition Manufacturers' Institute. Like Fannye Cook, Leopold had started observing and collecting wildlife as a child. His books *Game Management* and *Sand County Almanac* are classics in the field.

Leopold had made the game survey in his native Iowa and in Michigan, Minnesota, and Ohio, but he wanted to assess the situation in a place unfamiliar to him. Mississippi was chosen as a test because it had no statewide game department and a wealth of hunters.[20]

Aldo Leopold in the Pascagoula bottomland, December 1928. He was invited to do a comprehensive game survey of the state.

Aldo Leopold with his dog Flick in the Pascagoula River Bottomland during a 1928–29 trip to Mississippi.

Aldo Leopold roasting quail at his campsite along the Pascagoula.

He understood, as did many others, that an alliance between conservationists and hunters was a necessity, especially in a state with "a widespread and intense popular interest in game and hunting." Leopold cites many negatives in Mississippi's game situation: a decrease in wild turkey, quail, and deer, no refuge system, and little law enforcement of the existing weak game laws. On the other hand, he points out, "Mississippi excels any other state so far surveyed" in hunting interest. "The capitalization of this interest . . . is the only hope for maintaining a game supply in the face of the process of industrialization now underway throughout the South."[21]

Fannye Cook was involved in Leopold's survey, as their correspondence indicates. Leopold visited Cook in her home in Crystal Springs after his camping trip on the Pascagoula River. In a letter to her on January 6, 1929, he writes, "I hope to call on you at Crystal Springs about January 14. In case you do not plan to be there at that time I would appreciate you letting me know. . . ." Though his trip was delayed by two days, he did spend time with Cook before he returned home, and they must have walked around Lake Chautauqua, on the outskirts of Crystal Springs.[22]

On January 28, 1929, in a three-page handwritten letter to Leopold on Mississippi Association for the Conservation of Wild Life letterhead, she writes of the "Partridge-berry which you noticed in the woodland near Lake Chautauqua." She writes of a visit to the "hawk-killer" whom she couldn't persuade to bring her dead hawks so that she could examine the contents of their stomachs. She wants the rewards being offered for dead hawks to be discontinued. She apologizes for the delay in helping him with the financial report and will get the information to him at "the earliest possible date." She reports that she has had the flu and is "still getting two egg malted milks a day and am gaining strength rapidly." She concludes this letter by saying that "the bird's-eye view you gave me of your plans for future work was inspirational," and she hopes that he "may realize definite and satisfactory results from every effort expended."[23]

Cook's next three-page letter to Leopold came after she had seen his final report. Only a few carbon copies existed, and interested conservationists were passing them around. Cook says she has "marveled at the fullness of it" and trusts that the "institute may see fit to extend your services in these parts so that we may have more of your helpful counsel." She reports that she was never able to determine what the hawks were really eating, but that the Board of Supervisors of Copiah County had repealed the bounty on hawk heads.

Ever so diplomatically, Cook makes a correction in Leopold's report. On March 14, 1929, she writes, "Is it I who gave you the impression that bounty was given in Copiah County on cotton rats? If so, I'm sorry; because so far as I know, no bounty has been given or discussed." She closes by thanking him for the "privilege of looking over your report" and that she's mailing her copy to Mr. W. H. Smith.[24]

Leopold promptly answers this letter saying he has crossed the cotton rat bounties out of his copy and thanks Cook for license income information she has sent him. He writes again on December 27, 1929, to thank her for "the literature showing your continued activities." He indicates the possibility of locating "field grounds to demonstrate methods of quail management" in either Vinita, Oklahoma, or Holly Springs, Mississippi.[25]

Fortunately for future generations, we no longer have to rely on a few carbon copies. The Mississippi Museum of Natural Science has published a clear, bound edition of Leopold's report with helpful related documents such as maps and pertinent correspondence. Also included are pictures of Leopold with his dog Flick hunting woodcock in the Pascagoula Swamp and roasting quail in the woods.[26]

Fannye Cook's work continued as executive secretary for the Mississippi Association for the Conservation of Wild Life. Her annual report for the year 1928 says the convention was in Meridian on July 14 and that the executive committee met three times during the year, once in Meridian and twice in Jackson. Much of the report concerns the need for funding. The attorney general had issued an opinion that county boards of supervisors could legally make donations for conservation out of the sale of hunting licenses after the game wardens and their deputies were paid. Members of the executive committee appeared before several boards of supervisors and five responded with money. In Copiah, Bolivar, and Jones, the funds were used for educational programs: "Illustrated lectures were given in all schools, before the County Educational Associations, service clubs, Boy Scouts, and other organized groups."[27]

Cook addressed boards in Walthall, Pike, Lincoln, and Washington counties and "conferred in person with members of Tunica, Madison, and Scott Boards." Though she uses the passive voice and says that "talks have been made," she probably made most of them herself before garden clubs, Exchange clubs, Rotary clubs, Business and Professional Women's clubs, American Legion posts, and other organizations. Nature study was conducted with 4-H camps and Girl Reserves camps. Descriptions of the various contests encouraging conservation follow.

The association lobbied all Mississippi delegates to the US Congress to vote for the Federal Migratory Bird Refuge Bill, "the most important piece of wild life conservation legislation passed by that body in many years." President Coolidge signed the bill into law on February 18, 1928. Cook reports that Senator Pat Harrison introduced a bill to locate a federal fish hatchery in Mississippi, but says the association can do nothing to help at present.

The executive secretary ends her annual report on a note of frustration: "At times it has seemed impossible for the Executive Secretary to continue pushing the work of the Association forward with hardly enough funds for incidental expenses." She laments that they miss opportunities to advance their cause because of lack of funds.[28]

The 1929 annual meeting was in Jackson on July 19, Cook's fortieth birthday. Her invitation urges members to come and "carry home a renewed conservation spirit." Registration would be at the King Edward Hotel with a noon luncheon for one dollar. Members were asked to look over the program and decide which group meeting they want to attend. They were to invite their supervisors, game wardens, and representatives from their local sportsmen's clubs to come as well.[29] The energy and organizational, writing, and speaking skills that Cook invested in the Mississippi Association for the Conservation of Wild Life are evident in these documents.

The next month Cook is interviewed by the *Jackson Daily News* while she sits "Indian fashion on the hillside near Camp Kickapoo." She speaks of her work as her "very life" and that it was through her studies in ornithology at George Washington University that she became so interested in the flora and fauna of Mississippi. She says:

> It never dawned on me until this time that there was any great danger of certain birds, animals and flowers being exterminated in Mississippi, but I have found that many of the rare species are rapidly going and that each year this state looses [*sic*] thousands of dollars that they could save if they but knew how by establishing a state conservation department.

Cook goes on in the interview to elaborate on the dire conditions in the state. Streams and lakes were being dynamited or limed and fish were fast disappearing. People were killing hawks and owls, not realizing that most of their diet consists of rats, mice, and insects and that few take chickens. She talks about her first fair exhibit through the help of W. H. Smith of Laurel, head of the State Fair Association. She says that she brought her "precious little bird skins out of their cases and . . . exposed them to the dust of the fair."

Toward the end of the interview, Cook lists her conservation memberships in addition to the Mississippi Association for the Conservation of Wild Life: American Game Protective Association, American Ornithological Union, American Association of Mammalogists, American Nature Association, and the Torrey Botanical Society.

The journalist concluded the interview by asking Cook how she survived with no pay for all her work. Cook laughs and says, "Well, I stand in pretty good with the family and when I get hungry, hang my feet under my Dad's table. If I fall out with him, I go visiting."[30]

Birds of a Feather

Meanwhile, far away from Mississippi, another woman was waging her own battle for conservation. In many respects, Rosalie Edge and Fannye Cook were vastly different. Edge was born in New York City in 1877 to wealth and privilege, her family's apartment overlooking Central Park. She traveled throughout the world, was a suffragette, married a wealthy man, bore two children, and was later estranged from the husband, though they never divorced. Her interest in conservation began with bird-watching, though she did not become an activist until she was in her fifties.

Edge came later to conservation than did Cook, and her style was confrontational, earning her labels like "Common Scold" and "Hellcat."[31] She took on the Audubon Society when she discovered they were complicit with the Louisiana Department of Conservation's policy of allowing widespread trapping within the wildlife refuge. The society split thousands of dollars of profit from pelts with the trappers.[32]

Edge is best known, however—as indicated by the title of her biography, *Rosalie Edge, Hawk of Mercy: The Activist Who Saved Nature from the Conservationists*—for establishing a hawk sanctuary in Pennsylvania. In October on the Kittatinny Ridge, *sparebenbarich* (a Pennsylvania Dutch term) had become a tradition. This was the wholesale slaughter of thousands of hawks as they attempted to migrate south. Edge raised the money to buy the ridge, named it Hawk Mountain, and hired a caretaker. At her instruction, he posted "No Trespassing" signs for those with guns and charged fifteen cents for those who wanted to view the migratory spectacle.[33]

Fannye Cook probably knew about Rosalie Edge, her flamboyance, her lobbying of Congress, and possibly Edge knew Cook. Both were featured in a 1946 article in *Independent Woman*.[34] Both were sensitive to the fate of hawks, both knew Aldo Leopold, and both were members of the Wilson Ornithological Society.

In 1940 Cook attended a Wilson Ornithological Society committee meeting in Louisville, Kentucky. Also in attendance were Rosalie Edge, Amelia Laskey, and Margaret Nice, all women of distinction in the field of ornithology. It is interesting to imagine a conversation among these four quite different women, all with a passionate devotion to the cause of conservation.

A lifelong friendship began when Cook asked fourteen-year-old William H. Turcotte, who would later write, with David L. Watts, the definitive *Birds of Mississippi*, to make a talk at a program she had organized. She knew about him because he had a license to own collections of birds and bird eggs,[35] a license he would keep in his wallet for the rest of his life.[36]

Bill Turcotte and Fannye Cook were true birds of a feather. Turcotte had begun his obsession with birds at the age of six in Clinton, Mississippi, when nobody could identify a flock of starlings in the front yard—not his grandfather or his teachers at school. Finally a professor at Mississippi College identified the birds for him, and he began trying to identify every bird he saw and robbing nests. At age twelve he got his license to collect and would credit Cook with leading him to choose wildlife conservation as his profession.[37]

On March 11, 1931, Cook writes Dr. Bartsch on association letterhead that is much more elaborate than the early one. Centered under the title is in all capitals, "Fannye A. Cook, Executive Secretary." It claims 286 charter members with a box in the left margin listing the officers and executive committee, among them Mrs. W. D. Cook of Forest, Fannye's brother's wife. Next is a drawing by Nelson White of a hunter with gun uplifted toward ducks in flight. Then a final box states the objects of the association: "To stimulate interest in conserving native plants and animals for their economic and aesthetic value and to advocate the establishment of forest and wild life preserves for educational and recreational purposes."

In this letter Cook writes that she anticipates some "important conservation developments in Mississippi during this year" and that she is hopeful that her research program will be part of them. She goes on to say that "our purple martins came on Feb. 16 this time, much the earliest record I have." She adds that already this week she has made ten talks on birds, last week fifteen. "So you see I realy [*sic*] am doing work of a kind."[38]

Cook was correct in thinking that her long-worked-for goal would be achieved, but it was still a year away.

Landmark Year, 1932

The first good sign that the time had come for conservation laws in Mississippi was in 1932 with Governor Mike Conner's inaugural address, in which he called for the creation of a game and fish commission.[39]

That same year Lucy Howorth was newly elected to the Mississippi House of Representatives. Speaker Bailey made her chair of the Public Lands Committee and also assigned her to the Conservation Committee. Howorth came with a rich legacy; her mother, Nellie Nugent Somerville of Greenville, had been the first woman elected to the legislature when women were given the vote. The *Jackson Daily News* reported that Somerville and Howorth were the first mother-daughter team in the country to be elected to a state legislature.[40] Howorth had a brilliant mind; she was a skilled debater and an able politician. Her appointment to these committees was an auspicious one in furthering Cook's cause. The two were much alike—smart, focused, determined.

In addition to Howorth, the House of Representatives had two other female representatives that year—Madge Quin Fugler and Mildred Spurrier Topp. Topp was also assigned to the Conservation Committee, and Howorth was made secretary. Generally, Howorth did not like to be secretary of committees because she felt the role was often a lesser one assigned to women, but she welcomed the role with the Conservation Committee. She knew that, in the absence of the chairperson, she would be ranking member, and she was often floor manager as a result.[41]

Howorth's Public Lands Committee established a system of state parks and authorized the federal government to create national forests and parks within Mississippi.[42] And in the Conservation Committee, she, along with sixteen other House members, sponsored House Bill No. 116 establishing a state game and fish commission. The bill provided for the appointment of a commissioner for game wardens, for hunting, fishing, and trapping licenses, and for the conservation of the state's animal and plant life.

February 1932 must have been extremely stressful for Cook. In a letter on February 8, C. E. Lilly of the Mississippi State Fox Hunters Association says that he's sending her the names of over 150 hunters for her petition and will help her conservation efforts in any way he can because "if there is any state in the Union that is in need of such an organization, it is Mississippi." He says the game laws in his county are "absolutely worthless" "with no pretense at enforcement of them." And should her dream of a state commission become a reality, "the state can thank *only* you."[43]

Cook responds on February 16, saying she had wanted to answer sooner but explaining, "[I] lost my brother-in-law after wiring you last week and have needed to give my family much of my time and attention."[44] George Dodds Moody, husband of Cook's older sister, Alethia Belle, had died on February 11.[45] Cook goes on to say that she is "assured by our friends in the legislature that we are to have favorable committee reports on our bill. We are very hopeful of getting a good vote on the floors of both bodies."[46]

The bill passed the House on March 1, 1932. Among the nay votes was a member who voiced a perennial complaint—lack of funds: "I vote 'No' for the reason I doubt there being enough money in fund to pay enforcement officers, much less for conservation purposes," he said. Nevertheless, the ayes had it, and the bill went on to the Senate.[47]

The bill establishing the Mississippi State Game and Fish Commission passed the Senate and became law on March 9, 1932.[48] The cause for which Fannye Cook had dedicated seven uncompensated years of her life had come to fruition. We can only imagine her sense of relief, satisfaction, and joy. Now, at the age of forty-three came the question, what next? One would logically believe that she should have a top job at the commission, having dedicated herself so completely to its creation, and that she must have been denied that job because she was a woman.[49]

Cook sought the advice of her mentor at the Smithsonian, Paul Bartsch, "Curator of Mollusks and Cenozoic Invertebrates." In a handwritten letter on Mississippi Association for the Conservation of Wild Life letterhead and dated March 23, 1932, Cook tells Dr. Bartsch that the bill has passed and that she is sending him a copy of it. She goes on to say that she has

Governor Sennett Conner signing the Game and Fish legislation to establish the first statewide game laws in 1932.

been told she can have any job she wants, but on that decision she seeks his advice. She has considered commissioner of the southern district, but that's an unpaid, honorary appointment, and having "given [her] entire time without compensation since 1926 to the promotion of the conservation cause," she must have a paid position. As for being state conservation director, she thinks she would not like that position because of "all the enforcement problems." She goes on to say that she thinks she would be happier and do her best work in the areas of research and education and wonders, is "Director of Research and Education" an appropriate title?[50]

Dr. Bartsch responds from the Smithsonian on April 9, 1932. He says her letter has given him "considerable food for thought" and that he has been "digesting it and going over it a second time" and concurs that the best fit for her is "Director of Research and Education." And though agreeing with her decision, he follows with a paragraph that may well have annoyed her:

> If you were a man, any of the statutory positions would answer, but women are difficult problems to place (of course you won't like that, but the fact still remains and we have to face it). You can't change a woman into a man by fiat and probably if we could, we would prefer to have them as they are. But I think as Director of

> Research and Education you would do a splendid work for your state, and, what's more, you are eminently qualified to undertake that work, so good luck to you.[51]

The first commissioners appointed were Ben Stevens from Richton, W. E. McIntyre from Brandon, and W. G. McGill from New Albany. They were given office space in the New Capitol, but had to borrow fifteen hundred dollars to begin operations. They focused on three areas: administration and law enforcement, restoration and restocking, and education and public relations. The first director of conservation was Hunter Kimball. Fannye Cook was hired, not as "Director of Research and Education," but as "research assistant" on Sept. 7, 1932.[52] Had she been a man, no doubt "Director of Research" would have been hers. In some correspondence Cook would use the title "Research Secretary," but "Director" as title would not come her way until the museum was established.

Months after the victory of the bill's passing, Cook's mother, Martha Ellen Pierce Cook, died on January 31, 1933, at the age of seventy-six. Her death was surely a sad loss for the large, close Cook family. In late August of 1933, Cook writes Dr. Bartsch that she will arrive in Washington in early September and hopes to arrange a meeting with him to "talk over some matters." She writes on Mississippi Game and Fish Commission letterhead with an address and names of the director and commissioners listed but not her own. She was probably seeking his advice on the direction of her work.

Her English major and the ability to write well would stand her in good stead. A press release on November 25, 1933, was prepared by Cook, and distributed under the direction of Hunter Kimball, state director of conservation. The release explains that the disappointing duck hunting season, based on reports of the sixty-five conservation agents, was due to the long drought and to the lack of food for the ducks. The article goes on to describe measures that would-be hunters can take to accommodate the waterfowl, such as building dams to create lakes and thereby increase the fish population. Hunters are instructed to "shoot fair," and to make every effort to retrieve the birds they have wounded. This copy was probably sent to Bartsch. Cook's initialed handwritten note at the end says, "My plants came several weeks ago and I'm enjoying them week-ends."[53]

The year must have been bittersweet for Fannye, suffering the loss of her mother but experiencing the satisfaction of being launched in her career, a career which she would have to design.

SIX

The Great Depression and the WPA, 1934–41

> They [WPA workers on the Plant and Animal Survey] have become aware that conservation is a duty of all citizens and that it is also a form of religion, in that it creates a respect for and regard of God's handiwork.
>
> —Fannye Cook

Conservation in Washington, DC

A report in Fannye Cook's files from the United States Senate dated January 25, 1934, demonstrates that she remained well aware of what was going on in Washington, DC. The report is in the form of a letter to Franklin D. Roosevelt and lists the agreements reached when the Conference of Conservationists met with the Senate Committee on Conservation and Wild Life Resources. Agreements included funds to establish wildlife refuges and treaties with Canada and Mexico to conserve migratory birds. Among those listed as attending are Rosalie Edge representing the Emergency Conservation Committee and Aldo Leopold of the President's Committee of Three. While no Mississippian is listed personally, I. T. Quinn from Montgomery, Alabama, represented the Southern Association of Fish and Game Commissioners. Given her background and interests, it is possible that Fannye Cook attended this hearing.

Meanwhile, another Howorth, Judge Lucy's husband, Joseph, became a player for Cook. After several officials of the State Game and Fish Commission were unable to attend the 1936 North American Wild Life Conference in Washington, DC, she appointed Joe Howorth, living with Judge Lucy in the Roosevelt Hotel in Washington at the time, to be a delegate because, as

This is thought to be Fannye Cook in a canoe she made. The canoe is mentioned in a letter to Cook from Joe Howorth.

he said to program chair W. E. McIntyre, he was "very much interested in the conservation movement."[1]

Along with the letter to McIntyre, Howorth wrote a personal one to Cook that same day, one that illustrates not only Joe Howorth's engaging personality but Cook's as well. He writes to thank her for appointing him a delegate to the conference and then adds the following:

> What you told me about your building the canoe when I stopped by your office interested me very much. When the canoe is completed, when do you plan to make an exploration trip in Mississippi, and what river or creek would you explore? It may be that I would make application to make this trip with you. You will need a good paddler, as well as someone to help with the baggage and equipment and cooking. Do you plan to begin at the source of any stream? So many of our good streams are clogged with trees this might call for a lot of detours, tho many of the creeks and rivers ought to be open to a canoe for miles and miles. Such a trip would afford a wonderful opportunity to study the fish and birds of a stream. I think the best method of traveling with light equipment is to carry sleeping bags instead of a tent. The members of the "Wanderbirds" a hiking club of Washington, use and recommend this equipment as well as other items for light travel. If you are interested in the equipment used by them I will get more information about it for you.[2]

Whether the intended canoe trip took place remains a mystery, but the letter shows Cook and Howorth both to be avid naturalists who would not have minded the discomforts of a canoe.

Three years later the subsequent passage of the Federal Aid in Wildlife Restoration Act (known as Pittman-Robertson) in 1937 was good news for conservationists nationwide and would come to Fannye Cook in the midst of her WPA project. A historian of the program describes its passage as "a story of how cooperation gets things done, how States, the Federal Government, private conservation groups, and the sporting arms and ammunition industry joined hands to give Uncle Sam the best wildlife management scheme in the world."[3] Funds collected by an excise tax on the manufacturers of rifles, shotguns, ammunition, and archery equipment would be passed on to the US Fish and Wildlife Service.[4] Even today, this act provides a major source of funding for the Mississippi Department of Wildlife, Fisheries, and Parks.

Representative A. Willis Robertson added language to the bill making it impossible for states to take fees hunters paid for their licenses and use them for purposes other than administering the state game and fish departments.[5] Senator Pittman's bill was passed quickly by the Senate, but Robertson's committee lacked the jurisdiction to shepherd the bill through the House, and the bill was turned over to a committee headed by Scott Lucas of Illinois that delayed its passage.[6] Finally Carl Shoemaker, a conservationist and lawyer from Oregon who was often called the father of Pittman-Robertson, was called in.[7] Shoemaker "sent telegrams to all the garden clubs and women's groups in Illinois, urging them to contact Lucas on the matter."[8] Shoemaker said later when he ran into Lucas in the hall outside the congressman's office, Lucas threw up his hands and said, "For God's sake, Carl, take the women off my back and I'll report the bill at once."[9] The bill passed on August 17 and President Roosevelt signed it on September 2, 1937.[10] All the states eventually enacted laws that prohibited using hunting license fees for anything other than the operation of the wildlife agency. This made the states eligible for Pittman-Robertson funds.[11]

Organize for Education

Though employed by the state, Cook continued her work with the Mississippi Association for the Conservation of Wild Life. Her letter to Senator

P. W. Allen of Indianola, Mississippi, congratulates him on having been elected to the presidency of the organization at the annual meeting in July 1934. Cook says that after the conference she had been "taken very ill" and spent time in the hospital with "a bad kidney." She is sorry she has not congratulated Senator Allen sooner and thinks he is "the best man in Mississippi to direct the work of this organization." As a member of the executive committee, she offers her help in any way possible.[12]

The several references in her letters and papers of Cook's hospitalizations and various ailments make the enormous energy and drive she exhibits throughout her career even more remarkable.

In August Cook writes Senator Allen that she is sending him a copy of the resolutions passed at the annual meeting. One that needed the most immediate attention was the petition "to the Board of Trustees of High [*sic*] Learning, asking that they make conservation a required subject in all state schools doing teacher training courses." She suggests that Allen write to each of the advisors of the Mississippi Association for the Conservation of Wild Life and ask them to write the Board of Trustees.[13] Fortunately Mr. W. H. Smith served as secretary of the board and was also a former president of the Mississippi Association for the Conservation of Wild Life.

Apparently this appeal to the Board of Trustees was not successful, because in September 1934, Cook writes Senator Allen that she is "very sorry that the college board was not able to put on one or more trained conservation instructors this year, but it will be quite a step forward if we can get all the colleges working on this matter this session and keep the board interested." She goes on to say that she has collected catalogues from the colleges that offer teacher training and that she's enclosing suggestions of "something practical" on the subject of wildlife conservation that the presidents could incorporate in the curricula. She asks that Senator Allen write the presidents these suggestions because she has "so little time because of the various duties that are mine."[14]

Cook's dream of a state wildlife museum was years away, but in the fall of 1934, a friend donated to the Commission the museum's first taxidermy specimen for exhibit—a white-tailed buck with head and feet attached. The buck was sent to St. Louis for mounting. Cook recalls that other first specimens included "a striped bass from the Pascagoula River, a ground hog from northeast Mississippi, and an otter from Wayne County."[15]

Fannye Cook's duties would get more complicated and demanding as the nation sank deeper into the Great Depression. She would need a place to live in Jackson. What serendipity that Cook found a home with one of the nation's finest writers, one who offers us valuable glimpses into our conservationist's life.

Though the Great Depression "was not a noticeable phenomenon in the poorest state in the Union" as Eudora Welty wrote,[16] still it found many families taking measures they would not have expected. In the thirties, Welty and her mother Chestina took in Fannye Cook, sometimes with Vivian, sometimes with Rita, as boarders to make ends meet. The 1940 US census indicates that living in the Welty household at 1119 Pinehurst Street were Mrs. Welty, age fifty-six, Eudora, age thirty, her brother Edward, age twenty-seven, Fannye Cook, age fifty, and Vivian Electra, age forty-eight.[17] Beginning in 1936, both Welty and Cook went to work for Franklin D. Roosevelt's Works Progress Administration, Welty as a junior publicity agent (who fortunately carried her camera)[18] and Cook with the Plant and Animal Survey of Mississippi. Welty traveled the state writing press releases and documenting the human face of the Depression era; the Cooks were attempting to document every plant and animal.

The State Game and Fish Commission was one of the first in Mississippi to submit a project to the WPA in 1936. It was designed by Fannye Cook with this stated purpose and these objectives: "to provide employment for needy, professional, educational, and clerical persons; to assist the Game and Fish Commission in a plant and animal survey in order to determine the occurrence, distribution, relative abundance, and economic importance of species growing wild in Mississippi." And they proposed that this information be "made known to citizens of the state and to science."[19]

Cook writes Bartsch about the WPA project proposal, promising him more shells and including her four-part extremely detailed "narrative justification" for the project, along with forms on which the workers would report. The first part, Division A, focuses on determining "the occurrence, distribution, and relative abundance" of all the plants and animals in Mississippi and preparing specimens of them for study and research. Then she enumerates the many benefits of such a process as locating "wild plants suitable for transplanting to public parks and right-of-ways to make these more attractive to the public and to wildlife by providing food, cover, and nesting sites for wild birds and mammals."[20]

Division B is concerned primarily with birds and proposes to enlist school groups to construct, out of native materials, bird houses, feeding trays, and bird baths according to suggestions from such agencies as the US Biological Survey. "However, originality will be encouraged in designing and finishing." The educational component is extremely important because, though a rural state, very few of its citizens appreciate the flora and fauna and how important they are "in their relation to each other and to man in his pursuit of agriculture, forestry, and recreation." By way of example, she continues, "It is not uncommon for boys in all parts of the state, in nearly every community, to shoot birds of all kinds (except the mocking-bird). . . . They have not been taught to recognize birds or to appreciate life in nature."

That Cook was ever the teacher is reflected in a memory of Mrs. Halla Jo Ellis of Jackson. Mrs. Ellis's family had married into the Cook family, and her aunt Mrs. Halla May Patterson Turner (who served as secretary to the Senate for many years) was a good friend of Miss Cook. Mrs. Ellis recalls going with her aunt to the Old Asylum building in 1936 when she was nine years old to visit Miss Cook. Cook opened some of the drawers in her collection cabinet and told the child she could look at the birds' eggs and nests there, but must not take them out. Mrs. Ellis attributes this experience to the beginning of her lifelong interest in birds and in wildflowers.[21]

Division C has to do with the design and production of posters and nature booklets to be used in the schools and deposited later in libraries: "The value of nature booklets and poster work in influencing conservation has long been recognized in states where conservation has progressed."

Division D sees to "arranging time and place for conservation lectures to be given in schools, clubs, camps, and picture theatres; and assisting with lecture and picture programs to be supplied cooperating agencies, and sponsors of projects."

"Picture programs" were apparently very popular, judging from an article in the *Jackson Daily News* with the title "State Game Program in 'Reel' Style." A "four reel sound picture of the commission's work will be shown without cost to the throngs visiting the fair," the article promises. Accompanying the films would be exhibits in the game and fish building. Though this effort clearly had Cook's hand in it, she is never mentioned. An all-male cast appears in the film—a Native American gives a conservation lesson to a white man and Edgar W. Wright, a colonel and commissioner of Centreville, explains. Governor Hugh White has a speaking part as do chairman W. E. McIntosh, secretary Ben M. Stevens, colonel Reuben R. Banks of Columbus, George C. Weathers of Greenville, and director Si Corley.[22]

Division E focuses on "collecting and preparing local material suitable for museums, securing desirable places in public buildings for the display of materials collected and arranging displays." Each county will have a museum "to be open to the public free at all times during business hours, and on Sundays when possible."

Cook's plan was approved by the WPA, and cosponsors at several state colleges were alerted. Interestingly, in 1936 Cook's fellow Mississippian, Ellen Woodward, was serving as director of the Women's and Professional Division of the WPA. Fannye enlisted her sister Vivian Cook in this project, and work began with monthly reports sent to the regional director in New Orleans. The state was divided into four districts, and charts indicated the specimens collected, prepared, and classified in each district, as well as the number of conservation lectures, picture shows and exhibits, and groups served.[23]

A letter to Bartsch from Cook in early 1937 was answered by the "Assistant Curator of Mollusks," Harald H. Rehder. Cook is apparently well launched into the project, and Rehder identifies some of the specimens she has sent for help in identifying, as well as advice on the best way to catalog and label shells.[24] A curt letter to Cook from assistant secretary A. Wetmore begins, "In reply to your letter of June 22, I may say that Doctor Bartsch tells me that he has explained to you previously that the Museum has published nothing on the classification of mollusks. Our papers have dealt chiefly with small groups, but nothing that would be of help to you in your region." Wetmore goes on to write, "The best I can do is to report what he has said before," that he would name specimens Cook might send "in return for the specimens."

Cook's article "Mississippi Plant and Animal Survey" in the *Journal of the Mississippi Academy of Science*[25] demonstrates that she was an able historian as well as a writer and scientist. She traces the history of attempts toward a natural history survey, beginning with an act of the legislature in March 1850 entitled "An Act to Further Endow the University of Mississippi." Leadership went to a professor there and was subsequently passed to others in the state.[26] These early surveys were inconclusive and incomplete. In the early twenties "this writer" having observed "drought, fires, game hogs, unlicensed trappers, and many other destructive agencies," resolved "to do something about it" in the form of "a biological survey and a program of conservation education."[27]

The writer was as good as her word. A report in February 1939 shows that the project was operating in thirty-four counties with ninety-eight workers employed; 11,721 specimens had been collected, 9,364 prepared, and 7,015 classified. Conservation lectures numbering 1,681 had been given, 204 picture shows and exhibits displayed, and 3,467 groups served.[28]

Headquarters for the project was the abandoned state hospital building on North State Street,[29] also called the Old Asylum. Departments of Biology at Mississippi colleges served as cosponsors for the project, providing work space and becoming the homes of wildlife museums or dioramas built from the WPA collections and art.[30]

The final report is dated February 6, 1939–September 15, 1940. Fannye Cook is listed as technical supervisor; Vivian Cook as state supervisor and report compiler. Pages of typewritten text are followed by ten pages of snapshots with each corner secured with tabs as in a scrapbook. The pictures show the survey processes: surveying and collecting, cataloging and arranging, reproducing plants and animals with plastic molds and casts, and creating habitats. In addition, a chart of procedures includes taxidermy, museum art, photography, carpentry, compilation of data, and education. The data that follow indicate an enormous amount of work including 28,732 fish, reptiles, birds, plants, amphibians, and mammals collected. Miss Fannye A. Cook is quoted as saying,

> It has been no small task to train and re-train workers to whom the advanced and extremely careful work of a biological survey could be entrusted. Except for the optimistic and determined spirit in which most workers have accepted their assignments and except for the systematic cooperation of the WPA officials and cooperating biologists, the survey and other project plans could not have been executed.[31]

One such WPA worker in Mississippi was Maud Kendrick Lilly, born 1875 in Columbus, Georgia. Her parents moved to New York City when she was a child, and she grew up in that city and in Boston and studied art and music. She moved to Mississippi in 1895, married, was widowed, and in 1936 became art teacher for the Lee County Adult Education Project of the WPA. There she taught large art classes as well as individual lessons. She also painted studies of "anything Nature may offer . . . birds, hawks, snakes, fishes, wild flowers, wild berries, trees, shrubs, foxes, raccoon, possum, etc."[32]

Gordon Vaiden from the Delta, an amateur ornithologist with a bird egg collection, enlisted fourteen-year-old Sammy Ray to help him on the WPA project. Sammy's father had come from Syria when he was fourteen and later ran a store with barbeque in Rosedale, Mississippi, where Sammy was born. Vaiden gave Sammy a taxidermy book and a shotgun, and offered to teach him taxidermy and pay him $38 a month to help with some projects. Thus began a lifelong interest in wildlife. Ray ultimately earned a doctorate at Rice University and was a professor at Texas Agricultural and Mechanical University, Galveston, in the area of marine biology. Vaiden introduced him to Miss Cook. "I was impressed that she was a woman scientist," he said; "women didn't do things like that."[33]

Another WPA worker was Bill Turcotte, to whom Cook had taught basic ornithology and the correct method of preparing "study skins." Turcotte's job with the WPA was taxidermist.[34] Other field collectors included Henry Owens, R. M. Freeman, Homer L. Tackett, B. A. Bloodsworth, H. C. Robinson, C. D. Turnipseed, Winston Nolan, James Batson, and W. D. Lewis.[35]

Though Vivian Cook is listed as report compiler in their final WPA report, the last paragraph of this document was undoubtedly written by Fannye Cook because it exemplifies the evangelistic zeal that she felt for nature, a surprising presence in a technical report:

> Many of those privileged to work on this ambitious, cooperative program have developed a greatly changed attitude toward life and their environment. They have become aware that conservation is a duty of all citizens and that it is also a form of religion, in that it creates a respect for and regard of God's handiwork. They have derived genuine pleasure from seeing their own handiwork enjoyed and used by school children and the public in the attractive museums which have been built by these projects.[36]

State Wildlife Museum

Cook's next hope after the completion of the WPA project and the small displays on college campuses was that "a State Museum . . . be constructed in the Capital City at an early date to properly house growing state collections of natural history, art, and archives."[37] The first specimen for the eventual museum exhibits was the white-tailed buck that had been donated back in 1934, followed by a striped bass, a ground hog, and an otter.

One of the forerunners of a permanent museum was a mobile unit made up of glass cases containing wildlife displays from the WPA surveys. The truck held explanatory posters as well as a projector and conservation films. Films were unusual in the thirties in rural Mississippi and were of great interest. Cook writes, "For several years this truck went on a prearranged schedule to hundreds of communities throughout the state, where the exhibit was opened to visitors and motion pictures, with conservation appeal, were shown in the schools and local clubs."[38] She goes on to write that "a new truck was equipped with improved exhibits as an extension service, but was soon wrecked and the exhibits demolished."[39] As if to say, time for a permanent home. But because the commission was not able to acquire a space large enough for all the exhibits, the museum would move almost as many times as Cook did herself in her early years. She writes, "A room at the corner of Pearl and Congress Streets was used to display some of them."[40]

More enthusiastic about this space was the *Jackson Daily News*, which on January 1, 1939, carried an article entitled "Unique State Museum Opening Here," accompanied by a picture of an exhibit featuring nesting pelicans with an inset of a wild turkey. The museum was housed on the ground floor of the State Game and Fish Commission's new home at Pearl and Congress. An open house would be held on January 3 with the commissioners present. Taxidermist Frank Tobin had prepared the pelicans in their nests collected from North Island on the Mississippi Gulf Coast. Other exhibits featured herons, wood ibises, wild turkey, quail, horned owls, and barn owls. An aquatic display was also part of the museum offerings with toads, frogs, and water moccasins.[41]

Cook writes that some of the exhibits were displayed later in the halls of the War Memorial Building, but that many exhibits stored at the state fair grounds were seriously damaged by floods and weather.[42]

Finally all of the exhibits were brought together in the Old Asylum building on North State Street, which had served as headquarters for the WPA project. Cook writes that the building was condemned but that "the exhibits were renovated and opened to the public during office hours."

She goes on to write that "curatorial duties consumed much of the time of the staff" (presumably Cook herself), but the time left "was spent chiefly in preparing and mimeographing bulletins on the habits and economic importance of the species, represented in the study collections by approximately 16,500 specimens."[43]

Cook writes a more positive version of the museum in the Mississippi Game and Fish Commission's monthly publication. Her article begins with the headline "Down-Town Museum Becomes One of Show Places" and says that in the first month visitors have come from thirty-two Mississippi towns and seven states. Children from all the public schools have come. Several radio programs have already been broadcast and "arrangements have been made to broadcast a short program each Thursday at 3:15 p.m." She gives credit to the State Game and Fish Commission and the WPA for cooperating in making the exhibits possible. She ends the article by describing the latest table exhibits showing the diamondback terrapin and the softshell turtle, which are both "of great economic importance. Both of these reptiles appeal to the taste of the epicure, and are persistently sought by commercial fishermen and others who seek to supply the demand of leading restaurants."[44]

The museum would not move again until 1956, two years before Fannye Cook's retirement.

SEVEN

Work Continues in the War Years, 1941–45

What each of them had wanted was simply *all*.
—Eudora Welty

When the attack on Pearl Harbor in December 7, 1941, plunged the country into war, Eudora Welty began work on the short story "A Still Moment."[1] In this story—the only story of Welty's whose characters are historical figures—Lorenzo Dow, the evangelist, John Murrell, a serial killer, and John James Audubon, a naturalist, encounter each other on the Natchez Trace. Dow is riding a race horse at top speed toward his next camp meeting. To him the "voices in the throats of the wild beasts" seemed to turn into words that said "Praise God," and the birds sang "Peace in peace."[2] Murrell joins him, and they ride together with Murrell telling a long story about a silent man who has committed many acts of evil. Then finally Murrell intends to reveal that the silent man is himself and then murder Dow. The two come to "a great live oak tree at the edge of a low marsh-land"[3] when Murrell stops Dow's horse and each dismounts.

Audubon was coming toward them. In his walk he had tried to count a flock of purple finches that flew over him and to spell the sound of the ivory-billed woodpecker. He knew that animals had made the Trace "before man ever knew where he wanted to go."[4] The three men met and at that moment a "solitary snowy heron" flew down and began to feed near the marsh.[5] The men were transfixed by its beauty. To Dow the bird was the love of God made visible. To Murrell it symbolized his planned Mystic Rebellion when an army of slaves and outcasts would follow him, unfurling a banner of the

Devil. Audubon felt the "old stab of wonder." Welty describes this transcendent moment:

> What each of them had wanted was simply *all*. To save all souls, to destroy all men, to see and to record all life that filled this world—all—all but now a single frail yearning seemed to go out of the three of them for a moment and to stretch toward this one snowy, shy bird in the marshes. It was as if three whirlwinds had drawn together at some center, to find there feeding in peace a snowy heron. Its own slow spiral of flight could take it away in its own time, but for a little it held them still, it laid quiet over them, and they stood for a moment unburdened.[6]

But the still moment is broken when Audubon raises his gun and shoots the heron. When he picks it up, he sees that the bird is female, "just as one sees the moon as female,"[7] and he puts it in his bag and walks away. He knows that he cannot paint the bird from memory, that he must have its body to accurately represent it.

In her biography of Welty, Suzanne Marrs sees in Murrell the figure of Hitler.[8] It is also likely that Welty saw parallels in Audubon and Fannye Cook and her desire to document all—all the plants and animals of Mississippi. And her willingness to shoot the animals she loved in an attempt to save them.

Another Welty short story from that same year, "The Wide Net," may also echo the Cook-Welty association. A group of men, children, and dogs walk down the old Natchez Trace to the Pearl River: "Every step they took among the great walls of vines and among the passion-flowers started up a little life, a little flight."[9] The story is rich in such descriptions of the natural world. The purpose of the walk is to drag the river looking for the body of Hazel, wife of the main character, William Wallace, also the name of Cook's great uncle, brother to the Fanny Cook for whom she was named.

Did Cook read Welty's fiction? Perhaps. With her love of her flower garden, Welty was interested in Cook's reading material in at least one instance. She writes John Robinson that "Miss Cook has some old botany magazines from England 1837ish, bound copies that I have been enjoying."[10]

Another glimpse of Cook is in another letter Welty wrote to Robinson, who was serving in the Air Corps as an officer in North Africa and Sicily.[11] Welty called this account "Miss Cook's revenge":

> You know she is our roomer, the Fish and Game lady. Her offices are in the Old Asylum building, which is also occupied by the Highway Patrol and the FBI. Frances (Miss Cook) hates men. One day she heard a scratchy noise in the room next to her offices and found a man in it. She asked him the meaning—he said he was quite new, and they had only told him to claim it for his dark room. She didn't know, when I asked Highway Patrol or FBI—both annoy her. So she said she sometimes uses this room for a laboratory herself and if he wanted a darkroom she would suggest he clean out a room down the hall, which was packed to the ceiling with pamphlets (couldn't find what kind) and had a toilet and lavatory in it. "You can use it for dual purposes," stated Frances to this man. But the next day, scratchy noises again. So that night she went out and by way of a comment she put "38 or 40" of her largest specimens, in the room next door, in the sink and hanging over, and said if he should try again to occupy this room she thought they "would be sufficient." She told us what she had done in a very mild, scientific way—sort of like a report.[12]

As writers will do, Miss Welty exaggerates with the "Frances hates men" line. Cook loved her father and brothers as well as any number of male friends. But when they interfered with her work, they became a problem.

The next month, March, Welty writes to Robinson in some detail about how all the rivers have been flooding, and then about Cook's trip to the coast to greet the wood thrushes:

> Miss Cook awoke us at an early hour to announce the wood thrushes had arrived. Mother said, "Well, it certainly was raining." You know she goes out in a boat to meet them when they come in from S.A. out from Gulfport. Scouts (man or bird I don't know) tell her when. The birds all light on the boat and on her, they are so tired they don't move. They hitch hike in on Miss Cook's boat & Miss Cook. She observes them at close range. She invited me but I do not like things lighting on me, I'm almost sure.[13]

Welty was so taken with this image of Miss Cook's voyage that she recounts it again years later in a letter to Margaret Millar. Millar was married to Ken Millar, who, under the pen name Ross McDonald, wrote mystery novels. Ken and Eudora had become good friends; Ken and Margaret lived in California and were avid bird watchers. Margaret had published a book entitled *The Birds and the Beasts Were There*.[14] In her account of a bird-watching class she took, Margaret tells Eudora of a Mrs. Marie Beals who joins the class and clearly is an expert. She's taking the class because she had recently moved from Long Island to California and was interested in the birds there. It turned out that Mrs. Beals had banded more than fifteen thousand birds in her place on Long Island.[15] Welty writes, "When I read 'Beals,' I thought 'Cook,' like a password exchanged." She goes on to explain:

> She [Fannye Cook] began and ran the Wildlife Museum, just about on her own. She used to keep an annual appointment in the Gulf of Mexico with the birds returning from South America—she'd go out in a boat past the farthest bit of island, and so she herself—an old maid sitting up in a row boat not missing a thing—would be the first landing spot the birds would see, and they'd light all over her and be too tired to know her from a post—she gave them water and banded many, and had them come back again and again to her hands.[16]

Patti Carr Black, historian, writer, and longtime director of the Old Capitol Museum, recollects stories Welty told years after the Depression about her boarder and those WPA days. Miss Welty was fond of her boarder and amazed that a woman she saw usually in dresses and hose also had a "wild" side. Cook's large and caring family, members who would sometimes appear in hunting clothes, were "exotic" to Eudora. One night at dinner with Black and Charlotte Capers, Welty told how she never knew what she might find when she opened the refrigerator. She might find baby hawks in the bathtub or an owl in the refrigerator. And when she answered the phone, a voice might say, "Tell Miss Cook that Mr. Tackett is out of the swamp."[17]

The year 1942 brought another blow to the Cook family with the death of their beloved patriarch, G. M. Cook, on February 23 at the age of ninety-four.

As the war raged on overseas, Fannye Cook continued to collect specimens, work at the museum, and publish her bulletins. Paul Bartsch surfaces again in a series of letters in 1942–43 in which he thanks Cook for sending him her "Survey Bulletins on Alligators and Lizards of Mississippi"; she writes back that she is sending him another one because the "stapling machine was inadequate" in the first one: he responds with thanks and season's greeting on January 4, 1943.[18]

In June of that year Cook sends Bartsch two more bulletins, one on snakes and one on game animals. She types on Game and Fish Commission letterhead with the subhead "Pittman-Robertson Project, Mississippi 3-R":

> If, after looking over these bulletins, you think them to be of educational value to the general public as well as helpful to the biology departments of our schools and colleges, it will be appreciated if you will so state in acknowledging receipt of them to the Director of Conservation, State Game and Fish Commission. Also, any constructive criticisms which you may offer will be valued.

She closes the letter by hand: "Kindest personal regards."[19]

As we have seen, Cook was writing as well as collecting during those years. The library at the Mississippi Museum of Natural Science catalogs her bulletins published by the Game and Fish Commission. Many are based on data collected during the WPA project, and some have been hard bound and made available in public libraries. Several Pittman-Robertson projects are included.

In her 103-page *Game Birds of Mississippi* (1945), Cook writes in the foreword that:

> The bulletin has chiefly to do with distribution, life histories, habits, range, population status, importance as game, conservation requirements and measures taken to protect and increase the supply of various game birds that inhabit Mississippi, whether permanent residents, winter residents, or migrants stopping on spring or fall migration.

A letter to "My dear Miss Cook" from Paul Bartsch thanks her for his copy of *Game Birds*, which he will take "to the farm . . . to look it over in detail." The letter is signed:

> With the best of wishes for continued fine service, I beg to be,
>
> Appreciatively yours.[20]

Cook's hundred-page *Fur Resources of Mississippi* tracks the trapping statistics for raccoons, mink, muskrat, skunks, civet cat, weasel, opossum, beaver, otter, gray fox, red fox, and bobcat. The bulletin's detailed tables include documentation on the number of trappers, the number of pelts taken, the amount received from sales, and the rank of each county in the fur industry. The purpose of this information, as Cook writes in the foreword, is "to serve as a basis for recommending legislation for further protection and practical management of fur animals, and for the development of the fur industry in Mississippi."[21]

Again Paul Bartsch writes to thank Cook for his copy and to express his surprise that the fur bulletin follows "so quickly on the heels of the bird part." He goes on to say, "I think you are doing a splendid piece of work. Too bad they did not put in all that you had for the bird volume." He expresses surprise at the "value of the fur trade in Mississippi; that is certainly an item that should make the powers that be sit up and take notice and support your endeavor." He expresses his sympathy "when it comes to dealing with the fish problem" and writes that he looks forward to seeing how she deals with it. He ends by asking her to "receive my compliments and appreciation, and accept my congratulations. Truly yours."[22]

While Cook was an avid conservationist, she had a practical side which led her to consider hunters and industrial interests in her research and writing. The end of World War II would see no slowing in Fannye Cook's fight to preserve the natural resources of her home state.

EIGHT

War's End, 1945–49

[She never married because she had] a love affair with Nature.
—John Phares

When World War II came to a close, Cook continued to run the museum, to collect and document creatures from the natural world, and to prepare bulletins based on her research. Welty writes John Robinson, who would never permanently return to Mississippi, that "a baby fox has spent the night in our house (Frances's). He just crawled in a sack. He didn't even bark. What next? He was gray. Never saw the stars as bright as last night (I was waiting for the little fox to bark)."[1]

Years later Welty recollects that she once "helped her hunt for a baby bat in the window curtains, and found it. She asked for a little warm milk, fed the baby bat from a medicine dropper, and then I saw a baby bat belch. It was not quite as long as her thumb, and looked like something out of Hell—I'm glad it's not a bird."[2]

Fannye Cook is often remembered in an oral history project that Wiley Pruitt recorded in 1991 with retired persons from the fish and game world in preparation for his master's thesis, "The Best of All Breathing: Hunting and Environmental Change in Mississippi, 1900–1980."[3] In one interview, John Phares remembers hearing that Cook was in the Delta with a game warden and spotted a duck she wanted. The warden wouldn't go get the duck. It was cold and he didn't want to get wet, so Cook "stripped down to her teddies, said 'turn your back,'" and "went out there in her step-ins and got it."[4]

Phares describes Cook as an "interesting old gal," and says he often visited with her at the museum. He compares her to Caroline Dormon in

Eudora Welty took this photograph of a bat she helped Fannye Cook remove from the curtains of the Welty home. Cook boarded in the Welty home for many years, beginning during the Depression. She moved out in 1955. Copyright © Eudora Welty, LLC; courtesy Eudora Welty Collection—Mississippi Department of Archives and History.

Louisiana, who, like Cook, never married because "they had a love affair with Nature." He notes that the museum was not in the same building as the office for the Mississippi Game and Fish Commission and felt that she was in a sense relegated to the back room. Cook referred to her salary as her "little stipend," and he wonders if she was treated differently because she was a woman. She told him once that there was "not a thing under the sun that a man can do that a woman can't do better." He says he "never heard of any opposition to her, never heard a bad word about her."[5]

"Miss Cook is no desk chair conservationist," an article in *Independent Woman* said about her and followed that assertion with this quote from Cook:

Cook in jodhpurs, her usual field clothes.

In collecting specimens throughout the state I have run into many interesting situations and have had many thrilling experiences. Wading through acres of swamp water infested with alligators and cottonmouth moccasins to reach heronries in which not only herons but Louisiana water turkeys, bitterns, rails, gallinules, grebes and other water-loving species were photographed or collected, gives rise to emotions of fear and exhilaration not produced by any other experience.

This early rising on an April morning in preparation for the quest of wild turkeys and the quiet entering into a mixed pine and oak forest at the head of a small creek fed by springs where the woodland birds have begun their morning chorus fills one with the ecstasy of living. A launch trip to the Mississippi Sound where several species of terns, the laughing gulls, the brown pelicans, and the black skimmers nest in large numbers is one of the rarer experiences enjoyed by bird lovers. Lest trips be made in vain, one must be familiar with the nesting habits of these species to know when to find eggs and young. One of the many

> surprises I have met with has been finding diamondback rattlesnakes hibernating with gophers (turtles to you, possibly) in a hole several feet underground.[6]

Roger Conant

Snakes were the subjects of a correspondence between Cook and renowned herpetologist-conservationist Dr. Roger Conant, curator of the Philadelphia Zoological Garden. Conant was a descendant of early settler Roger Conant, a leader in Salem, Massachusetts, and later the Massachusetts Bay Colony. Dr. Conant's *Field Guide to Reptiles and Amphibians of the Eastern United States* was first published in 1958 and has subsequently gone through three editions in the Peterson Field Guide Series. Conant published some 240 scientific papers and twelve books in his scholarly career.

Conant writes Cook on May 9, 1945, to congratulate her on her paper published in the current *Copeia.* He goes on to say:

> We have all suspected that *Lampropeltis* [*c.*] *calligaster* [Prairie Kingsnake] and *L.* [*c.*] *rhombomaculata* [Mole Kingsnake] would eventually be found to intergrade. (Note: Their ranges overlap in parts of Mississippi, Tennessee, and Kentucky.) Some years ago I examined a specimen from Kentucky (the first recorded in that state, incidentally) and Mr. Dury of the Cincinnati Museum of Natural History has gotten one or two others from Kentucky since then, I believe. All showed tendencies of intergradation but we didn't have enough material to prove it. You are doing some very good work down in your part of the country. Do keep it up.[7]

Cook writes promptly to thank him for his "heartening letter."[8]

A year later Conant writes to ask for help on his book on North American water snakes. He needs *Natrix erythrogaster* (Red-bellied Water Snake) and wants it alive. He will pay freight and send the shipping materials.[9] Cook responds that she is not currently doing field work, but thinks she can supply him with "a few specimens of *erythrogaster* and will try to get them to [him] alive." She goes on to say that she looks forward to the monograph when it's finished.[10]

Conant promptly responds with thanks and to say that he's sending her a copy of a paper on *Natrix valida.*[11] Three days later Cook writes to thank him and says she would like to have some more of his bulletins, particularly ones that pertain to species in her region.[12] Conant says that he will put her on his mailing list for further publications and asks that should she "be so extremely lucky as to find specimens" of *Natrix erythrogaster* or *Natrix rigida*, that she will "bear [him] in mind."[13] Cook writes to thank him and assures him that she will try to get the specimens he needs.[14]

Two years later, Cook writes to ask Conant if he is still interested in live specimens of the snakes:

> If you wish the live snakes shipped to you, please send me shipping material and instructions for the care of the snakes. Should they be shipped in the bags in which I place them in the field—putting the bags in a live box—or should they be turned loose in the box so that food and water could be given them by the express people in route?[15]

Three months later, Cook writes Conant and thanks him for "reprints relating to certain reptiles and amphibians." She expresses regret that she didn't get to speak with him on the trip down the Mississippi River that was a part of the New Orleans Conference of Ichthyologists and Herpetologists and has a question about one of their stops:

> I recall that at one place where we stopped on the trip down the Mississippi River (I believe it was in a marsh near the sulphur mine) a *Natrix* was collected and was at the time said to be *clarkii*. I understood some one to say that you retained this specimen. I should like very much to know if, upon further examination of the specimen, you are still of the opinion that it is *N. clarkii* [Gulf Saltmarsh Water Snake]. I seem to recall that it had a single row of dark spots forming a median ventral stripe as in *N. grahamii*. It is my understanding that *clarkii* is characterized by two clouded brown bands dotted with black along the abdomen.
>
> When you have a leisure moment, I would appreciate a note giving your final identification of this specimen.[16]

Conant responds that he is "much chagrined to learn that you were at the meetings in New Orleans and that you were one of the members who took the trip down the Delta." He would certainly have liked to meet her and talk water snakes. The questioned specimen was indeed *N. clarkii*. He suggests that perhaps Cook did not get a good look at the snake, but it had some small yellow spots that many of the specimens have. Should she find any *Natrix erythrogaster* [Red-bellied Water Snake] or its subspecies, he would like to see it, "preferably alive," and would pay the postage.[17]

The next year, Conant writes to thank Cook for her letter of December 21 and says he "shall be privileged to borrow some of the specimens from your collection." He is "swamped" at the moment as he finishes the revisions of the "Reptiles of Ohio," but she will hear from him in the future.[18]

Clearly the two remained in touch. In a 1969 article about snakes published by the American Museum of Natural History in New York, Conant cites both Cook's 1943 and 1954 snake publications. He writes, "Specimens that have been preserved for long periods of time or have been exposed to light tend to show more markings." This may account for Cook's statement[19] that one of her *lodingi* "approached" *mugitus*. (*Mugitus* could refer to *Pituophis melanoleucus lodingi*, or Black Pine Snake, and *Pituophis melanoleucus mugitus*, Florida Pine Snake; Black Pine Snakes are listed as "threatened" and are under consideration to be escalated to "endangered," due to rarity, according to the US Fish and Wildlife service.) "I have not seen this snake," Conant writes, "for it could not be found when Miss Cook very kindly sent me her material for study. Some of her other specimens showed marked evidence of fading."[20]

Fish became a focus of Cook's collecting in the later forties and early fifties and were the subject of more Pittman-Robertson funds which came Mississippi's way in 1945. Mississippi Game and Fish Commission letterhead stationary has the subhead Pittman-Robertson Project with Fannye A. Cook listed as "Project Leader." Cook writes Dr. S. F. Hildebrand at the Division of Fishes at the Smithsonian National Museum of Natural History to ask for photographs of "the different species of the game and possibly of the commercial fishes of importance and interest to sportsmen and fresh water fishermen in Mississippi."[21] She is preparing a "pocket folder" on the subject. She includes a long list with the scientific names of the fish pictures she would like.[22]

A reply came three days later from Leonard P. Schultz, "Curator of Fishes." He says that they don't maintain a file of fish "portraits," and that drawings make up the bulk of their files. Five days later Cook responds that perhaps she can get permission to reproduce some images from the bulletin of the Bureau of Fisheries and asks Dr. Schultz to keep her request in mind and should he run into any of the requested photographs in his "line of duty" to please send them to her.[23]

In 1948, Cook writes Dr. Hilderbrand, reminding him, "On April 17, 1934, I sent you for identification a group of minnows which Mr. Rheinhammer, a commercial fisherman with a house boat on Pearl River, at Jackson, brought into our office. The group contained two (2) darters which you identified as Log Perch, or *Percina caprodes*." Cook is now interested in comparing these log perch with one found in the Tennessee River drainage area and asks that he, "or someone," mail back one of the specimens she sent in 1934. She goes on to say that Hilderbrand, in his letter to her of April 26, 1934, wrote that he might have found some log perch in Eagle and Moon Lakes, and she would like to borrow those specimens "for a few days." She goes on to write that she had "been hoping to do some collecting early this spring, but the water remains high and is too deep for [her] to wade."[24]

Cook closes by saying she hopes that if Hildebrand is coming to the Annual Convention of the American Society of Ichthyologists and Herpetologists in New Orleans she will see him and that he will "plan to spend some time with [them] in Jackson, or on some of [their] lakes and streams."[25]

The letter speaks not only to Cook's knowledge regarding the fish world but to her meticulous record-keeping of her paper trail. Culmination of her fish project would be far more detailed than the "pocket folder" first envisioned, but it was still years away.

A letter from Harald A. Rehder, now "Curator of Mollusks" instead of Paul Bartsch, responds to Cook's questions about some fish flesh embedded with parasites that she had sent. Rehder had inquired of the Bureau of Animal Industry at the US Department of Agriculture. They write, "We would not, knowingly, care to eat such fish, but doubt if we would suffer any ill effects if we did, provided the fish was thoroughly cooked." They go on to identify seven species of Florida fish that have had this parasite reported.[26]

Cook was often accompanied by game wardens on her collecting expeditions. Gordon Strickland of Marion County recalled that Cook, "a fine ole lady," wanted to "seine all the creeks" in his county. He was a young man in his thirties at the time, Cook in her late fifties. "She'd get in that creek with me . . . I'd be wet, pulling that seine, she'd be wet. She'd put minnows in a jar. We never did get anything big enough to eat. She didn't back up from a alligator, cottonmouth or nothing. 'Strick, let's see what's in that hole right there,' and she'd study it. Dinner time she'd sit on a log with you and eat sardines and crackers. She know'd what she was about."

Mississippi Game and Fish Commission officer in early uniform with new vehicle.

Once a friend asked Strickland, "What you doing in them woods with that ole lady?" Strickland first told him "that comes under the head of my business" but then explained she was old enough to be his mother and was an outstanding person with Game and Fish and was completely safe with him. "I loved Miss Fannye Cook," Strickland said, "I respected her til her time come to an end."[27]

One of Strickland's biggest challenges was catching fishermen who were "telephoning" fish. This was the practice of lowering a telephone into the river to shock large numbers of fish to the surface to be gathered, surely an anathema to Cook. A favorite target was the flathead catfish in the Pearl River. Once Strickland spotted two boats in the river with "fine citizens" whose families were gathered at the camp for a big fish fry. He suspected what the men were up to, and he knew an old woman in the area was often out in a little wooden boat. He donned a disguise he carried with him that included a sunbonnet and a brassiere. He rowed out to check and found they were indeed telephoning.

"That's ole Strick," one shouted when he recognized the warden, and they promptly threw the telephones into the river. Strickland fished the telephones out of the water for evidence and fined the men. There was no fish fry at the camp that day. "I've arrested preachers, lawyers, doctors, even a fellow ran a restaurant in Hattiesburg." The Pearl River was full of flathead catfish, but they would not have lasted long if telephoning had been permitted.

Mr. Strickland offers many examples of the difficulties of controlling natural habitats. South Mississippi was depleted of deer when Strickland became game warden in 1948. "When I was a boy, I didn't know what a deer track looked like," he said. Game and Fish made a concerted effort to restock, with Strickland and others making seven trips to Wisconsin in five pickups, bringing deer back. Later, "headlighting" deer, the practice of shining bright lights into a deer's eyes to paralyze it, and then to shoot it, became one of his main enforcement problems. He would chase violators in his pickup, once catching the mayor of Pascagoula and his police chief at the practice.

Some twenty years later, he remembers a "terrible day" when deer had become so plentiful on Leaf River Refuge that they were starving. Game and Fish planned a deer kill with licensed hunters checking in. They figured that about 300 hunters would show up and around 200 deer would be killed. Instead, 3,200 men checked in, and at the end of the day 940 deer had been killed.

Beavers offered another challenge. Efforts to restock them were so successful that soon Game and Fish was called upon to break up beaver dams and remove the animals.

When asked if he thought Miss Cook was against hunting and fishing, Strickland said not at all, but in a controlled way. Would she be pleased with how the game and fish situation in Mississippi has progressed? He said, "She would be tickled to death to see we moved forward." But what she really hoped, he said, was that "it would all come back like it was when the Indians were here."[28]

Cook would collect many other creatures in the course of her career, but birds would remain one of the main subjects of her collections. John

Fannye Cook portrait that hung in the MMNS library for many years (known as the blue dress portrait).

Phares observed that she came along at a time when one "identified birds over the sights of a gun barrel."[29] But bird-watching and encouraging others to bird-watch was a focus as well.

One who often accompanied her on bird-watching and egg-collecting expeditions was Bill Turcotte. Their friendship continued while he was earning a bachelor of science in biology at Mississippi College. Bill's son John writes that, "while in college, he took a baby crow from the nest and raised it on dog food. The crow followed Daddy everywhere and would sit in MC classrooms and was known by the faculty so well that one of Daddy's professors included the crow in roll call. Daddy also raised several pet great horned owls."[30]

In fact, Bill Turcotte spent so much time driving Cook around on birding trips that it became an issue with Annie Cook Turcotte, whom he courted and married. She was not related to Fannye. Later, however, John writes, "Mama tolerated this after she realized that Miss Cook (who never married) was not romantically interested in Daddy."[31]

Eudora Welty went on a birding trip with Cook one Sunday morning across the Pearl River to a

> night-spot called, appropriately, First Place, and parked. Miss Cook said we were likely to see both red-eyed and white-eyed vireos. Well, sitting on the bench outside First Place were what I would call red-eyed vireos, left-overs from Saturday night, but Miss Cook didn't waste any time noticing them. She was stopped once by a road-block on the Natchez Trace where they were chasing an outlaw in the swamps, just where she was headed, and she told the fellows she had no intention of interfering with either them or the outlaws, and she would thank them not to interfere with her, she was looking for some birds, and she went right on. (She called all men "fellows.").... Miss Cook herself was very elegant and stern, strict, matter of fact, rather impatient with human beings.[32]

Clearly Welty was more interested in Fannye Cook's fearless character than in the birds they went to see. She makes no mention of seeing birds in the rest of the letter. She would later regret not having paid more attention since "the one and only state authority on [birds] lived in our house for 25 years, Miss Fannye Cook of Crystal Springs."[33]

NINE

Directing, Collecting, Organizing, and Publishing in the 1950s

She never had the opportunity she would have had if she'd been a male.
—Barry Freeman

In the 1950s, some twenty-five years after starting her campaign to save Mississippi's natural world, Fannye Cook reached the apex of her career. She would continue to direct the museum, collect specimens from nature, and maintain a wide correspondence with other scientists and scholars. She would organize another statewide organization. She would continue to publish her work.

Cook's great nephew, Bill Cook, remembers working on his Eagle badge with the Boy Scouts around 1950. His troop went to the museum for a "bird study" with Aunt Frances. He remembers the Old Asylum museum as "musty, awful, with all the plaster falling off." Aunt Frances had a reputation among the Scouts as being tough. She wouldn't sign off on their badge unless they had mastered the material. She told several of them they'd have to go back and study some more. Her nephew remembers her as "all business, not jovial, but kind, interested in what you were doing."[1]

An article in the *Jackson Daily News* on October 15, 1953, carries the headline "Museum Lady, Crusader for Conservation, Serves State." Officers of the Business and Professional Women's Club had cited Fannye Cook for recognition during National Business Women's Week. Cook is quoted as saying that "women of Mississippi played a very active role in getting conservation laws passed in this state."

The reporter describes a typical day for Fannye Cook:

Fannye Cook with white-tailed deer exhibit. This photo was published in the *MS Game and Fish* magazine in 1953 with a long story promoting the Wildlife Museum at the 111 North Jefferson Street location.

> A day with Miss Cook is likely to include several lectures to groups of students and tourists who visit the museum. She may prepare a nature activity program for a garden club, plan fair exhibits, answer voluminous correspondence on anything from lamprey eels to pileated woodpeckers. She may write a paper for a scientific publication or assist biologists in laboratory studies.

A picture of Cook with the museum's mounted deer accompanies the article.[2]

In 1954, *Snakes of Mississippi: A Survey Bulletin* by Fannye A. Cook was published by the Mississippi Game and Fish Commission. Her preface explains that this book is an update of a 1943 bulletin, one probably mimeographed by Cook and resulting from work on the WPA survey. She writes:

> It is believed that snakes have great potential value in maintaining a balance in nature, and that conservationists and farmers would profit by conducting local investigations to determine the extent to which snakes may be made to serve a useful purpose; and on the other hand, to what extent snakes may be locally detrimental to other species, the protection of which is desirable.

WPA Plant and Animal Survey bird taxidermist, Mr. Wiggley.

Bobwhite quail release in the early years of the Mississippi Game and Fish Commission.

Cook and Bill Turcotte attending an event at one of the first Mississippi state parks.

Vivian Cook (in black dress) and Bill Turcotte (in light jacket) attending an event at one of the first Mississippi state parks. Fannye Cook in background (in white shirt).

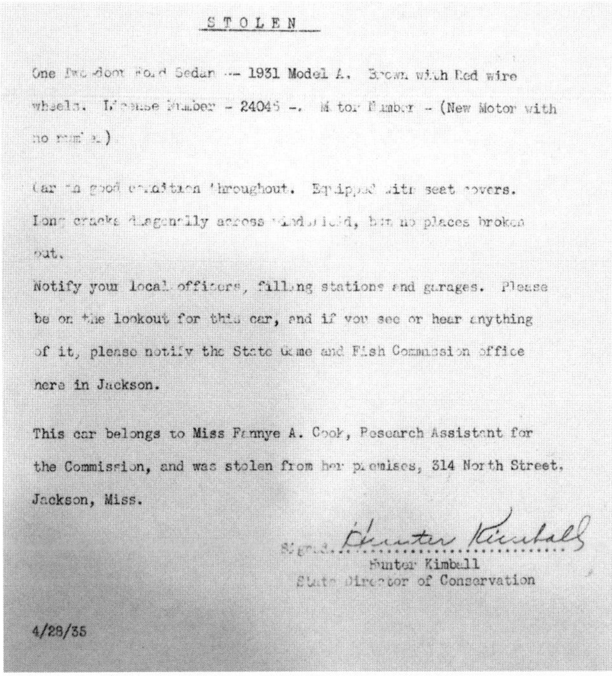

STOLEN

One Two-door Ford Sedan --- 1931 Model A. Brown with Red wire wheels. License Number - 24045 -. Motor Number - (New Motor with no number)

Car in good condition throughout. Equipped with seat covers. Long cracks diagonally across windshield, but no places broken out.

Notify your local officers, filling stations and garages. Please be on the lookout for this car, and if you see or hear anything of it, please notify the State Game and Fish Commission office here in Jackson.

This car belongs to Miss Fannye A. Cook, Research Assistant for the Commission, and was stolen from her premises, 314 North Street, Jackson, Miss.

Signed Hunter Kimball
Hunter Kimball
State Director of Conservation

4/28/35

Document concerning Cook's stolen truck.

Cook with an exhibit about beavers constructed by WPA workers in the State Wildlife Museum in Jackson.

Beulah Delano painting a plaster cast of a snake.

Ellisville WPA museum classroom.

WPA workers collecting specimens.

Fish and waterfowl poster made by WPA workers for statewide distribution.

Laboratory classroom in one of the nineteen WPA museums.

Legion State Park WPA museum.

WPA workers making plants for museum exhibits.

Museum exhibits in the Lauderdale County WPA museum at Meridian Community College.

North island, Chandeleur Islands, collecting trip. Turcotte (far left), Frank Tobin (second from left), R. M. Freeman (third from left), Fannye Cook (fifth from left).

WPA workers collecting plants on Back Bay, Biloxi.

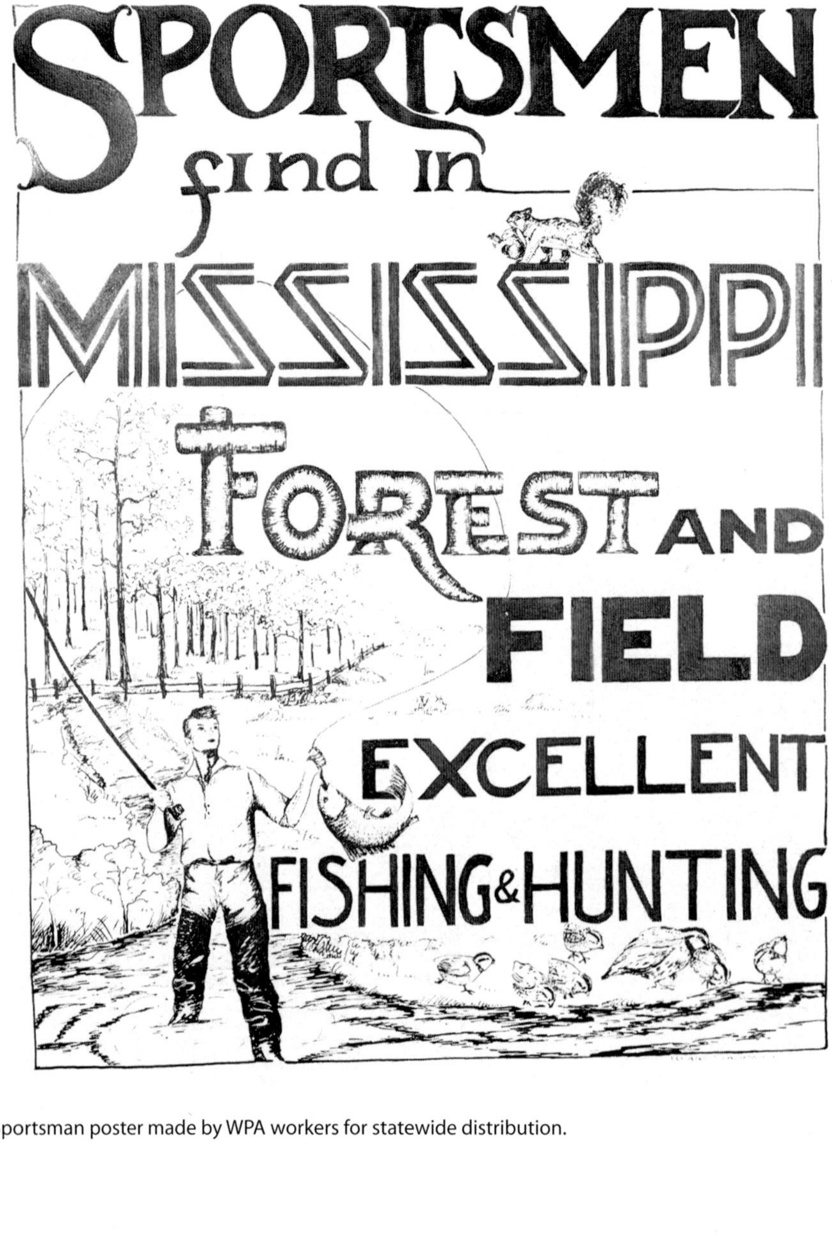

Sportsman poster made by WPA workers for statewide distribution.

Plant and Animal Survey record keeper.

University of Southern Mississippi museum classroom with professor. One of the goals of the survey was to make conservation education accessible throughout the state.

WPA crew working and camping in Pascagoula River swamp at Poticaw Landing. Left to right: A. Haelfrich, P. Hinton, F. Wiggley, M. Miller, Eli Miller, Old Dad (local trapper), Mr. Byrd (landowner), Mr. Love, and Mr. Weddle.

WPA workers painting dioramas for installation in the museums around the state. More than seven hundred paintings were produced.

WPA artists drawing habitat on one of the barrier islands in preparation of an exhibit.

WPA museum on Delta State College campus in Cleveland, Mississippi.

WPA workers preparing specimens in the field. More than twenty-eight thousand specimens were prepared for use in the nineteen museums during the Depression.

These artists carefully recorded habitat features and plants on the island.

Frank Tobin, taxidermist from the Field Museum of Natural History in Chicago, worked on many of the exhibits for the museums.

WPA workers making educational booklet. More than eighteen hundred booklets emerged from the surveys workrooms on subjects ranging from native plants to life histories of mammals.

WPA worker identifying insects for the systematic collections at the State Wildlife Museum in Jackson.

WPA museum at Mississippi State College for Women, Columbus, Mississippi.

The "Movie Truck" traveled the state with a film depicting conscientious hunters and fishermen obeying the new game laws. Maurice Burnham, shown here, brought films and a collection of animals to fairs and schools around the state to introduce people to the concept of wildlife conservation.

Museum artists working on diorama backgrounds.

Lauderdale county WPA museum at Meridian Community College.

Biology class meeting in the WPA museum at Copiah-Lincoln Community College.

Bird taxidermist at Copiah -Lincoln Community College museum.

Copiah-Lincoln Community College museum with WPA workers.

Beulah Delano painting plants at the State Wildlife Museum in Jackson.

This exhibit at a Jones County fair in September 1938 had more than forty thousand visitors. The exhibit was prepared by WPA Plant and Animal Survey workers at Jones County Community College in Ellisville.

This exhibit was on display at the Forrest County Fair and was prepared by the WPA museum at University of Southern Mississippi in Hattiesburg.

WPA worker, Frank Stribling, cataloging and identifying freshwater mussels at the State Wildlife Museum in Jackson.

Sammy Ray making an owl exhibit for the WPA museum at Mississippi Delta Community College in Moorhead.

WPA float made for a parade in Poplarville by WPA Plant and Animal Survey workers at Pearl River County Community College.

University of Southern Mississippi taxidermist, Mr. Wall, working on the museum exhibits.

Jones County Community College Plant and Animal Survey museum.

The book characterizes the forty-two recognized species and races in Mississippi and contains charts of their distribution by county. Cook would subsequently revise the book in 1962.

Throughout the 1950s, extremely technical correspondence with scientists at universities and at the Smithsonian indicate that Cook had not forgotten fishes. Detailed descriptions as well as specimens of fish themselves go back and forth through the mail.[3]

A record from 1955 shows that Fannye Cook collected a Chimney Swift (*Chaetura pelagica*) at 1119 Pinehurst Street, Jackson, the address of the Welty home. It was the last collection at that address because that was the year Welty wrote her literary editor friend Mary Louise Aswell, explaining that "Mother has put out our lady naturalist (& her owls) & moved downstairs, where she can have her own sitting room, bedroom & bath, & no stairs to climb."[4] Mrs. Welty was not well, their financial situation had improved, and clearly they needed their house back. Cook moved to 827 North State Street, next door to the Municipal Art Gallery, but often spent weekends at the home place in Crystal Springs with two sisters.[5]

Vivian Cook's home base was Crystal Springs as she traveled the state with welfare and social work. Lena Mae Brignac's husband had died of a heart attack right before Christmas in 1941, and Lena Mae moved to the Cook house in Crystal Springs, where she cooked and kept house for Fannye and Vivian and for other family members who visited, such as Rita and her husband Bill Bizzell.[6]

Birds are often mentioned as Cook's first love, and in 1955 she founded the Mississippi Ornithological Society and served as its first president. That year she helped the Nature Conservancy buy part of Horn Island in the Gulf of Mexico, the first step in the formation of the Gulf Islands National Seashore administered by the National Park Service.[7]

Two years before her retirement, Cook was able to move the museum from the Old Asylum building to a better location, as she writes in *Mississippi Game and Fish*:

> In April 1956 a new location for the Museum was provided at 111 North Jefferson Street. Here it has been possible to arrange the exhibits more attractively. Separate rooms have been set off for the collections. Visitors to the Museum are very complimentary of the exhibits. They find the quarters more comfortable and the free parking space ample and convenient. The exhibits continue to remain open

State Wildlife Museum at 111 North Jefferson Street. This wooden building was replaced by a new building in 1973.

> to visitors and the research material is made available to qualified students. Guide service is provided classes or other groups upon request. Requests for information and conservation material are taken care of daily. Specimens brought or sent to the Museum for identification are promptly identified and the desired information given. Boy Scouts who are frequent visitors to the Museum are given assistance in qualifying for merit badges in Nature Study and Conservation.[8]

John Turcotte remembers going with his father to the state fair and visiting the Jefferson Street wildlife museum, a wood frame building located across from the fairground entrance. He describes Miss Cook as resembling "the typical 1950's middle-aged schoolteachers who taught me at Clinton. She was a tall, long-armed, fit, modestly dressed, scholarly, and articulate person."[9]

Despite all the work at the Museum, Cook still went birding. John Turcotte remembers going birding with her and his father, trips which he did not enjoy:

> I remember following them once to see a Scarlet Tanager in Rankin County near Brandon at Legion Lake. During these outings, Miss Cook would stride along just

> as fast as Daddy, who was a rugged, athletic type man. They never seemed to get thirsty or hungry while chasing down birds. It was difficult to follow behind them because they would grab limbs in the way, which would spring back and hit me in the face.[10]

John says that his father's egg collection was, "for a long time, the only complete egg collection of every bird that nested in Mississippi. He and Miss Cook labeled, cataloged, and mounted each egg in cotton-lined walled enclosures in a wooden chest of drawers."[11]

Patti Carr Black remembers a joke that Charlotte Capers, then head of the Department of Archives and History, played on her when she first came to Archives and History as librarian in 1957. Capers told her that she wanted the two of them to go to the museum and learn from Miss Cook's card catalog. Black was, of course, expecting a well-organized group of drawers with a well-documented note card for each item. Fannye Cook gladly went along and showed them her catalog—drawer after drawer of dead birds.[12] Cook had extensive, meticulously written catalogues for all the collections as well. Museum director Libby Hartfield explains that the biological specimens are "now incredibly valuable of course because they give us the DNA from all these animals."[13]

Cook's great niece, Mary Elizabeth Smith, daughter of Jewell Cook Witherspoon and granddaughter of W. D. Cook,[14] was amazed by that "card catalog" and thought her aunt "was from another planet," but she was her "hero." Smith characterizes Cook as "funny, sure of herself, patient." And she "liked children." Smith has a young grandchild living in Austin, Texas, who shares that fascination with birds and other animals, and she hopes that he can one day be an intern at the museum, that he can follow in Aunt Frances's footsteps.[15]

Even Cook's failures could serve as inspiration. John Turcotte writes:

> Finally, I credit Miss Cook indirectly for my M.A. degree. Daddy did not get a Master's degree, and I believe neither did Miss Cook, although she did study on the graduate level. Daddy told me that this was one of her lifelong regrets as it was for him. He strongly encouraged me to get mine and mentioned Miss Cook's experience. Apparently, she had to work hard to establish her credibility with professors at all stages of her career and when attempting to publish her work. Daddy said that men tried to push her around and marginalize her, but she more

Cook spoke at the twenty-fifth anniversary celebration for the Mississippi Game and Fish Commission at Henneberry Wildlife Management Area in 1957. Rex Mc Raney, executive director of MGFC, stands next to her, and the young boy in the foreground is Phillip Strong Jr.

> than held her own. Knowing from my 40 years experience in state government, she must have been as skilled in political science as she was in natural science.[16]

In 1957 Cook published *Salamanders of Mississippi*, another of the survey bulletins based on the WPA collections. She is listed on the title page as museum director. She explains in the introduction that a key is given to help identify the six salamander families of Mississippi, along with

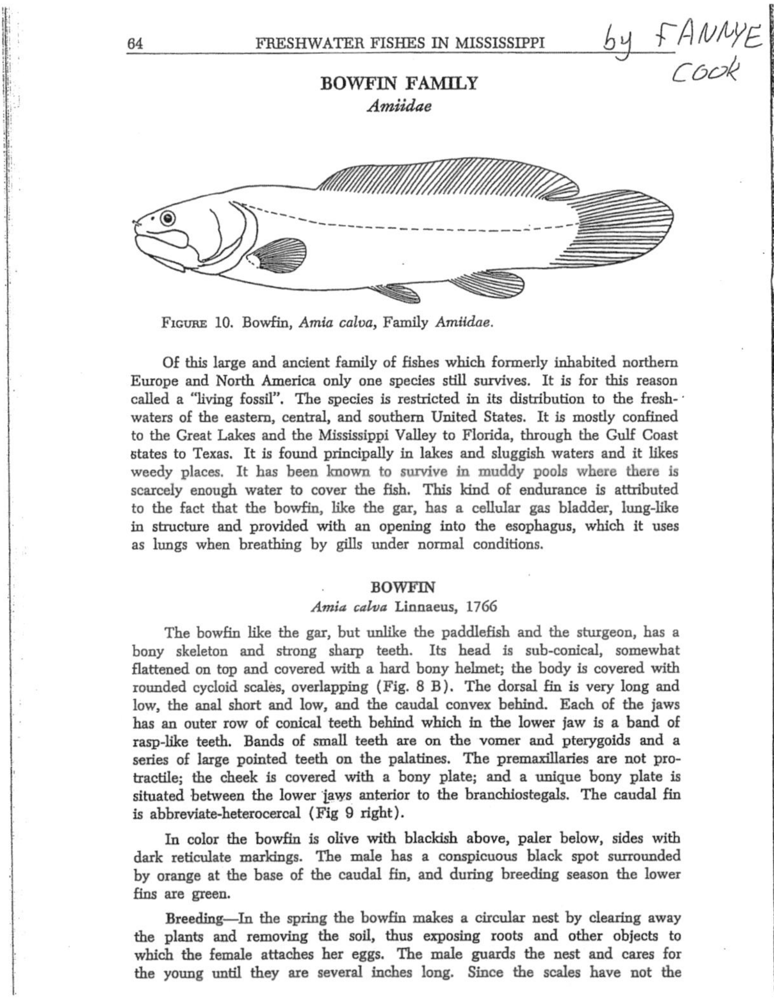

64 FRESHWATER FISHES IN MISSISSIPPI by FANNYE COOK

BOWFIN FAMILY
Amiidae

FIGURE 10. Bowfin, *Amia calva*, Family *Amiidae*.

Of this large and ancient family of fishes which formerly inhabited northern Europe and North America only one species still survives. It is for this reason called a "living fossil". The species is restricted in its distribution to the fresh-waters of the eastern, central, and southern United States. It is mostly confined to the Great Lakes and the Mississippi Valley to Florida, through the Gulf Coast states to Texas. It is found principally in lakes and sluggish waters and it likes weedy places. It has been known to survive in muddy pools where there is scarcely enough water to cover the fish. This kind of endurance is attributed to the fact that the bowfin, like the gar, has a cellular gas bladder, lung-like in structure and provided with an opening into the esophagus, which it uses as lungs when breathing by gills under normal conditions.

BOWFIN
Amia calva Linnaeus, 1766

The bowfin like the gar, but unlike the paddlefish and the sturgeon, has a bony skeleton and strong sharp teeth. Its head is sub-conical, somewhat flattened on top and covered with a hard bony helmet; the body is covered with rounded cycloid scales, overlapping (Fig. 8 B). The dorsal fin is very long and low, the anal short and low, and the caudal convex behind. Each of the jaws has an outer row of conical teeth behind which in the lower jaw is a band of rasp-like teeth. Bands of small teeth are on the vomer and pterygoids and a series of large pointed teeth on the palatines. The premaxillaries are not protractile; the cheek is covered with a bony plate; and a unique bony plate is situated between the lower jaws anterior to the branchiostegals. The caudal fin is abbreviate-heterocercal (Fig 9 right).

In color the bowfin is olive with blackish above, paler below, sides with dark reticulate markings. The male has a conspicuous black spot surrounded by orange at the base of the caudal fin, and during breeding season the lower fins are green.

Breeding—In the spring the bowfin makes a circular nest by clearing away the plants and removing the soil, thus exposing roots and other objects to which the female attaches her eggs. The male guards the nest and cares for the young until they are several inches long. Since the scales have not the

Bowfin drawing by Sam Gore for *Freshwater Fishes of Mississippi* by Fannye Cook.

descriptions. Measurements are "total length and length of tail." She further explains that "total length is the distance from the tip of the snout to the tip of the tail, and the tail length is from the posterior angle of the vent to the tip of the tail." Tables identify the counties in which the salamanders were collected and the museums on college and high school campuses in which they may be seen.

Fish would next occupy much of Cook's time as she prepared *Freshwater Fishes in Mississippi* for publication. No fish "portraits" appear in the book, but it contains a number of finely detailed drawings. Illustrator was Samuel Marshall Gore, now a noted sculptor, then a young art instructor at Mississippi College. Cook hired him for four dollars an hour. She knew about him because he had worked on the Game and Fish magazine. He remembers Miss Cook as a "perfectionist who would get out the magnifying glass to inspect my work." He had to draw using a magnifying glass. The drawings had to be to scale, and Cook would measure. He remembers the sound of Fannye Cook's glasses rattling against the eyepiece of a microscope. Sometimes he had to dissect a fish that had been in formaldehyde to get the specifics just right. He would smell like a fish and go home to find that his wife had prepared fish for supper. He remembers Miss Cook as "intelligent and smart." She was driving with him once when they passed a big dead tree. "There's beauty even in a dead tree," she said.[17]

Another of Wiley Pruitt's interviewees was Barry Freeman, son of R. M. Freeman, who served as director of the Game and Fish Commission from 1945 to 1952. Both father and son were biologists in the Fisheries Division. Barry Freeman remembers birds as Miss Cook's first love, and his father is listed in collection records as working with Cook in 1940 collecting birds in the Tombigbee River swamp.[18] Barry remembers going bird-watching as a child with Cook along the Leaf River. He later left the state and served as fisheries head in Florida. When he returned to Mississippi in 1955, he became head of the Fisheries Division and had more encounters with Cook.

"There wouldn't be a Game and Fish Commission if she hadn't come back from D.C.," he says in the interview. He says some people were quite critical of her. He remembers a fish study on Moon Lake when Cook appeared with a ruler to measure fish. A biology professor at the University of Mississippi criticized her methods and book. But Freeman protested that "she *did* fisheries, wading through water with snakes. He wouldn't do it. She never had the opportunity she would have had if she'd been a male."[19]

Collection records at the Museum indicate that Cook had started collecting fish in 1936, probably as part of the WPA project. Sometimes she is listed alone as the collector, and sometimes there were so many that the collector is listed "Cook, F. A. *et al.*" The years 1947–49 were particularly active in fish collection, and she was often accompanied by game wardens. The last in the record is the Mississippi silvery minnow collected by F. A. Cook from the Pearl River at the Wilson Bridge on April 19, 1958.

Fannye Cook's retirement party: far left, Cook; far right, Bill Turcotte.

Formal retirement would come for Cook before her fish book was published.

Retirement, 1958

After twenty-six years of employment by the state and thirty-two years after she began her campaign to establish the Mississippi Game and Fish Commission, Fannye Cook retired at the age of sixty-nine. Retirement was mandatory at seventy. An appreciation dinner in her honor and sponsored by the employees of the Game and Fish Commission was held on November 18, 1958, at seven o'clock, in the Arlington Room of the Robert E. Lee Hotel in downtown Jackson.

The dinner began with a song and a prayer, an appropriate beginning to celebrate the contributions of a woman for whom nature carried such spiritual power. The invocation was delivered by the Reverend Morelle H. Wells, pastor at Alta Woods Methodist Church, Jackson. Alta Woods was a new church, organized in 1952, with a permanent sanctuary that opened in 1956.[20] The Reverend Wells had served in Crystal Springs and probably knew Cook through that connection, and they had a great deal in common. Wells had traveled extensively in Europe and South America, and he was a vigorous hiker and backpacker.[21]

Master of ceremonies was Rex McRaney, executive director of the Game and Fish Commission. Elkin Jack, chairman of the commission, introduced the speakers. The first speaker was J. P. Coleman, governor of Mississippi, and the second was judge W. E. McIntyre Sr., one of the first three commissioners appointed in 1932. Special guests made remarks and then her old friend Bill Turcotte, chief of the Game Division of the commission, presented an honorarium. J. F. Stuart, assistant director of the commission, presented a tribute, the text of which was included in the program.

The tribute salutes Cook for her efforts in the establishment of the State Game and Fish Commission, for her scientific research and publications, and for her "guiding hands" that "developed and maintained with loving care our splendid wildlife museum." Pointing toward the future, the tribute concludes, "Your example of service above self, for work well done with vision, courage and relentless effort will inspire us to work to the extent of our talents."

On December 1, 1958, B. E. Gandy took over as director of the museum. He and Cook worked together for a month. Mr. Gandy remembers her as "extremely professional in every way."[22] He says he was young, "feeling his oats," and, seeing the number of organizations she belonged to and the amount of publishing that she had done, told her he had a family and didn't think he could be that involved. "You chose to have a family," Cook told him, "I chose to stay single and be professional."

Later he found a bird mislabeled. "We'll correct it," Cook told him. A few days later, he told her a warbler had been misnamed. Cook replied, "Mr. Gandy, I don't make mistakes on warblers. I'll answer your questions, but I'm trying to finish this book."[23]

At University of Southern Mississippi, Gandy became fascinated with the wildlife museum, its birds, and its big rattlesnake following a rabbit. It was one of the eighteen museums across the state Cook had established in connection with the WPA project. After majoring in chemistry and

B. E. Gandy, director after Miss Cook, 1958–1987.

biology, he taught school in Jackson and often visited the museum. He first met Cook when his students found a bird, and he took it to her for identification—a black rail, a rare, secretive, solitary bird.

Before she left the museum, Cook called a meeting of men active in Game and Fish—Turcotte, Tackett, Phares, Freeman—and introduced them to Gandy and told them to work together. "Then she did me a great favor," Gandy says. "She *left*. Left me with her secretary and maid."[24] Cook's official career had come to an end, but her work on behalf of Mississippi's wildlife was far from over.

TEN

The Work Goes On, 1959

Oh the gallant Fishers life
It is the best of any,
'Tis full of pleasure, void of strife,
And 'tis belov'd of many;
—Isaac Walton, 1653

To retire and go fishing is the dream of many folks, but for Fannye Cook, fish had a meaning far beyond the leisurely. Her goal during this first year of so-called retirement was to finish and publish her fish book.

Six months after her official retirement, Cook returned to the museum to ask Mr. Gandy if he might loan her his secretary, Mrs. Adele Jackson, to help with the book. Gandy kindly agreed, and Cook drove each day from Crystal Springs to work on the manuscript.[1]

Freshwater Fishes in Mississippi, published in 1959, is a remarkable book, bringing together Cook's years of scientific research and her clear writing style, Sam Gore's meticulous drawings, and H. L. Tackett's maps. In the Preface, Cook thanks a number of scientists around the country, including Dr. Samuel Hildebrand, who had also granted her permission to use his unpublished Mississippi work. She thanks Dr. Leonard Schultz and his staff at the Smithsonian National Museum of Natural History for providing "pleasant working conditions" and "many other courtesies" when she was there studying the Mississippi collections. Fish had evidently taken her to Washington a number of times. She writes, "Special thanks are due the game wardens and their supervisors who assisted so ably and willingly in collecting specimens from local waters and in otherwise expediting the

Cook photograph taken outdoors not long before her retirement.

field work." And she thanks Mrs. Jackson, whose work seems amazing in that pre-computer time.

In the preface, Cook hopes that the book might "serve as a basis for further study, as a reference in research, and as a handy key for identification of species found here." It undoubtedly has.

Cook's hometown newspaper, the Crystal Springs *Meteor*, ran a story about the book with the headline "Miss Fannye Cook Publishes New Book 'Fresh Water Fishes in Mississippi.'"[2] It notes that following the publication of her book, the American Association for the Advancement of Science declared Cook a fellow and sent her a certificate recognizing her as a scientist. Cook is "not only an authority on fishes, but is familiar with Mississippi birds, mammals, reptiles, and amphibians; and she has worked extensively with wild flowering plants."

Then the story reveals a little-known area of Cook's research. As a member of the Mississippi Genealogical Society, she researched old cemeteries and Bibles:

> Volume One of the Society's publications on Cemeteries and Bibles contains complete information from the stones in seventy-nine cemeteries in Copiah, many of which are old plantation cemeteries which have not been used for many years and are fast reverting to nature, carrying with them information which in some instances can be had from no other source.

The article ends with a picture of *Freshwater Fishes in Mississippi* and an editor's note that says certainly Miss Cook should have had her picture there, but she had told the editor that "anyone over 40 should avoid pictures."[3]

B. E. Gandy, in a conversation with Wiley Pruitt years later, remembered the obstacles in the early days of conservation to considering all species, not just those that could be killed and eaten. But, he said, "Miss Cook did it in her fish book, she covered all the species, not just game fish. She set an example."[4]

ELEVEN

The 1960s and the Last Walk

As Saint Francis of old made feathered friends,
So she, like-named, protectress came to be
To ev'ry winged thing.
—Dorothy Moore Alford

With fish off her plate, Cook continued to live her life built around the natural world. As the civil rights movement caught fire in Mississippi in the early sixties, Cook must have understood that a time for change in human relations was long overdue. We know that Eudora Welty was so moved at the assassination of Medgar Evers in June of 1963 that she wrote "Where Is the Voice Coming From?" The story was published in the *New Yorker* and made clear the mindset of one who could commit such a murder. And while we have no written record of Fannye Cook's thoughts on the civil rights movement, we can be confident that she supported equal rights for people just as she did for all of God's creation.

She did not participate in freedom marches, so far as we know, but was always willing to take people of all kinds on bird walks. Laura Bowers of Canton remembered such a walk in a conversation with Wiley Pruitt in 1991. Bowers had grown up in Canton and became interested in birds through her father and Miss Christine Berry, who taught English at Millsaps College. She met Bill Turcotte and Fannye Cook and knew Cook's brother Gilbert, who lived in Canton. She describes Cook as "not pretty, but striking, tall, with a distinctive way of walking."[1]

Fannye Cook grave in the Crystal Springs cemetery. Photograph by Libby Hartfield.

Later Bowers went to work for the Natchez Trace at the Tupelo headquarters. In spring of 1964 she learned that Fannye Cook would be leading a bird walk at Tishomingo State Park not far away. She drove over that morning where Fannye and her sister had spent the night in one of the small cabins. They waited around past the announced time, but nobody else showed up for the walk, and so Cook took Bowers on a walk over the limestone hills to a creek. They saw a colony of cliff swallows and the first Rose-breasted Grosbeak that Bowers had ever seen. Cook knew the birds not just by sight, but by their songs. Bowers says she was "walking on air" to think she was bird-watching with Miss Cook and cherishes the memory.[2]

A week later, Cook took a group of young people, possibly Boy Scouts for whom she was a counselor, on a bird walk. She died the next day, April 30, 1964, at the age of seventy-four.[3] Her obituary says she died in a hospital in Hazlehurst, not far from Crystal Springs, which did not have a hospital then. The funeral was at ten in the morning on Saturday at the Methodist church in Crystal Springs, with burial in the city's cemetery.[4]

So as Freedom Summer began in Mississippi, Fannye Cook left this life as she had lived it, sharing her love of nature until the end.

Remembrances

Not long after Fannye Cook's passing, a door slammed at the museum, startling Mr. Gandy. "Don't worry," Mrs. Davis, an employee, told him, "that's just Miss Cook checking in." And her presence is felt to this day.

The month following Cook's death, May 1964, the Mississippi legislature, under governor Paul B. Johnson, named the museum the State Wildlife Museum, the Fannye A. Cook Memorial. They also passed a resolution commending her for her contributions to wildlife conservation.[5]

On July 15, 1965, four days before what would have been Cook's seventy-fifth birthday, the Camellia Garden Club held a memorial service on the Lake Chautauqua grounds in her honor. The focus of the service was the dedication of a plaque, with dedicatory remarks by Mrs. J. D. Barron and acceptance by Mr. G. P. Cook, one of Fannye's older brothers. The Rev. J. R. Cameron gave a prayer, and Mrs. R. E. Alford a poem:

Dedication
(To Miss Frances Cook)

Life spoke to her from ev'ry branch and stream
As, passing, she gave ear to birds' delight
And gazed raptly into the darksome dream
Of peels with fins half-in, half-out of sight.
The wonders of Nature filled her being;
She thrilled to movement, to color, to sound;
With others she shared her gift of seeing
The bounty of God in the world around.
As Saint Francis of old made feathered friends,
So she, like-named, protectress came to be
To ev'ry winged thing whose joy depends
Upon its simple needs and flight full free.
Now is this lovely shrine established here
For birds and her, our friend, who held them dear.
Dorothy Moore Alford

Following the poem, the speaker was introduced by mayor L. W. Kitchens, and the speech was delivered by Mr. B. E. Gandy. The benediction was pronounced by the Rev. D. J. Benson.

Birdbath with Saint Francis in Chautauqua Park, Crystal Springs, in memory of Fannye Cook.

On March 29, 1967, a portrait of Miss Cook was presented by her family to the State Wildlife Museum, the Fannye A. Cook Memorial. The portrait had been painted by Karl Wolfe of Jackson. Karl Wolfe had been on birding trips with Miss Cook and spoke fondly of her according to his daughter, Elizabeth "Bebe" Wolfe:

> Being young at the time my parents were friends with Fannye Cook, I have no memory of ever meeting her, but she was a presence in my life, nonetheless. I well remember the many excursions to the Natural Science Museums—in their former locations, before the miracle of air conditioning, with my mother and my brother; peering into little drawers filled with bird skins and other strange and interesting treasures. My mother would tell me about Fannye, and her devotion to the study of the natural world. Even then I felt a bit envious of her for having the time and wherewithal to devote to the discovery of nests and eggs and other secret things—all of which fascinated me.
>
> My father's first cousin was Frances Wills, who was Fannye Cook's best friend. My parents socialized with Frances and her husband Willy. These gatherings were adult affairs, but as I grew older, stories were shared about how Fannye drove a Model T Ford long after they became antique, and she usually drove it in first

Fannye Cook's portrait by Karl Wolfe.

gear, because she didn't want to miss anything along the way. Sometimes she left it running—forgetting to turn off the ignition when she stopped in to see a friend and would emerge from the visit to find she'd run out of gas.

My father, Karl Wolfe, was commissioned to paint a portrait of Fannye. I don't remember when it was, perhaps in the 1960s. His reference was a black and white photo. I well remember the delight he took in bringing her to life on the canvas in full color, outdoors, with trees and birds in the background, and I also remember the real affection and admiration he felt toward her.

Through her friendship with my parents, she must have learned something about me as a child and my own love for nature. As she was retiring from her active life, she gave my father something she wanted me to have—a powerful magnifying glass mounted into a jointed brass stand. It's a very useful thing. I was astonished by her recognition of my young and passionate interest and have always felt grateful for this gift from a kindred spirit.[6]

B. E. Gandy presided at Cook's funeral. G. P. Cook presented the portrait on behalf of the family, and it was accepted by Billy Joe Cross, executive director of the Mississippi Game and Fish Commission. Her old friend Bill Turcotte gave a tribute.

Libby Hartfield, education coordinator (1978–1988) and director (1988–2015). Photograph by James Patterson.

After Cook's retirement and death, the museum would move twice more from the site where Fannye Cook was director. On November 9, 1973, a new building was dedicated across from the fair grounds and named the Mississippi Museum of Natural Science, the Fannye A. Cook Memorial. Gandy explained that the name "Science" was chosen instead of "History" to reflect continuing research and experimentation, not just a record of the past. That language is clearly in line with Cook's philosophy.[7]

In 1979 the museum was flooded, suffering extensive damage to the collections, many of which Cook had collected and mounted herself. Gandy recalled being in a boat, struggling to save as much as they could, despite the hopelessness of many of their efforts. The building was repaired on that site and in 1983 was threatened again by flood, but this time the gap had been closed in the levee and it held.[8]

At the end of this interview Gandy pointed out three important buildings close to each other in Jackson and all named for single women—the Eudora Welty Library, the Charlotte Capers Archives and History Building, and the State Wildlife Museum, the Fannye A. Cook Memorial. They were

Mississippi Museum of Natural Science. Opened March 3, 2000, in LeFleur's Bluff State Park. Photograph by Steve Saxton.

Atrium of Mississippi Museum of Natural Science in LeFleur's Bluff State Park. Photograph by Steve Saxton.

Large saltwater aquarium in Mississippi Museum of Natural Science. Photograph by Steve Saxton.

Ground sloth exhibit in Mississippi Museum of Natural Science. Photograph by Steve Saxton.

Images of Cook desk and objects displayed in an exhibit in MMNS. Photographs by Steve Saxton.

Typewriter that Cook used for many years.

"not limited by family," he concludes, and were able to devote themselves "totally to their work."[9] Evidence, he implies, that women can't have it all.

B. E. Gandy led the museum as director until his retirement in January of 1987. Libby Hartfield joined the museum staff as education coordinator in 1978 and became director in 1988.

In March 2000, the current Mississippi Museum of Natural Science moved to higher ground and opened at LeFleur's Bluff State Park in Jackson. The complex is a fitting testimony to its founder's vision. The ninety-seven-thousand-square-foot building sits on three hundred acres of natural landscape with 2.5 miles of walking trails and an open-air amphitheater. Inside the building are thirty thousand square feet of permanent exhibits, a seventeen-hundred-square-foot greenhouse called "The Swamp," a hundred-thousand-gallon aquarium network with over two hundred living species, a gift shop, and a library.[10] The core of its eighteen-thousand-volume library, Fannye Cook's materials, were donated to the museum in 1965 by her family. Cook's office remains as she left it and is on display in the museum.

In 2012, the museum opened an eighteen-thousand-square-foot expansion of its laboratory and collections space, which now houses over one million scientific specimens. The museum's mission statement speaks to Cook's insistence on the dual roles of scientific research and education: "The mission of the Mississippi Museum of Natural Science is to promote understanding and appreciation of Mississippi's biological diversity through collections, research, scientific databases, education, and exhibits, and to inspire the people of our state to respect the environment and to preserve natural Mississippi."

Libby Hartfield retired in 2015 and Charles Knight took the reins as the fourth director of the Mississippi Museum of Natural Science. The educational mission of the museum is being carried out in a number of creative ways, including teacher resources and workshops, family events, and Girl and Boy Scout programs. Hartfield, along with the museum staff, started a weekly radio program, *Creature Comforts*, to answer questions from those who call in or email about animals they see in nature. Along with the wildlife team, Dr. Troy Majure, a veterinarian, answers questions about home pets.

In the words of Gordon Strickland, what Miss Cook hoped for was that her native ground "would all come back like it was when the Indians were here."[11] No doubt Fannye Cook would have found her place in a pristine world of nature, with virgin forests intact and rivers pure and unpolluted. But she was an intelligent, practical woman who did not look back. She saw devastation and set her sights on ways to make her home state better for present and future generations. We can all be grateful to her for her insight and courage.

Appendix 1

List of WPA Museums in Mississippi

Copiah-Lincoln Community College, Wesson
Delta State University, Cleveland
East Central Mississippi Community College, Decatur
East Mississippi Community College, Scooba
Greenwood High School, Greenwood
Holmes Community College, Goodman
Jones County Community College, Ellisville
Legion State Park, Louisville
Leroy Percy State Park, Hollandale
Meridian Community College, Meridian
Mississippi Delta Community College, Moorhead
Mississippi State University, Starkville
Mississippi University for Women, Columbus
Pearl River County Community College, Poplarville
Perkinston Community College, Perkinston
Southwest Mississippi Community College, Summit
State Wildlife Museum, Jackson
University of Mississippi, Oxford
University of Southern Mississippi, Hattiesburg

Some lists also include Greenville, Clarksdale, and Meridian High Schools.

Appendix 2

The Object of a Biological Survey as Proposed for the State of Mississippi

To determine the occurrence and distribution of plants and animals in Mississippi, and to make known to the citizens of the State and to science the various species found.

To determine by working out life histories the feeding habits and movements of birds, mammals, and all the lower forms in order to arrive at a better understanding of their economic importance in relation to man, food and clothing, to crop plants, gardens, orchards, and forests.

To determine the kind and extent of damage done by harmful rodents, birds, and other forms and to advise means of checking and controlling such ravages.

To aid in the establishment of game reserves and advise suitable localities for the preservation of the different kinds of game, thus making it possible to restock areas already depleted.

To aid in the establishment of plant preserves for the protection of rare plants.

To cooperate with existing organizations in the prevention of fires and other agencies which destroy, not only feed, shelter, and nesting sites of birds and animals, but also millions of feet of timber, beautiful shrubs and flowers, thus robbing the State of her richest resources and priceless assets.

To prevent boys and irresponsible citizens from using insectivorous birds and other useful life as targets, and to put a ban on our dogs and stray cats which destroy eggs and young birds.

To advocate strict enforcement of all State and Federal game laws.

To collect and mount specimens representative of existing species found in the State to be exhibited in a place accessible to the largest number of visitors, and to prepare series of scientific study specimens to be retained at the A & M College for the benefit of natural science students.

To educate children and the general public in their appreciation and proper enjoyment of the natural things which make up their environment.

Appendix 3

Route Travelled and Location of Possible Research Agencies

Appendix (a-1)

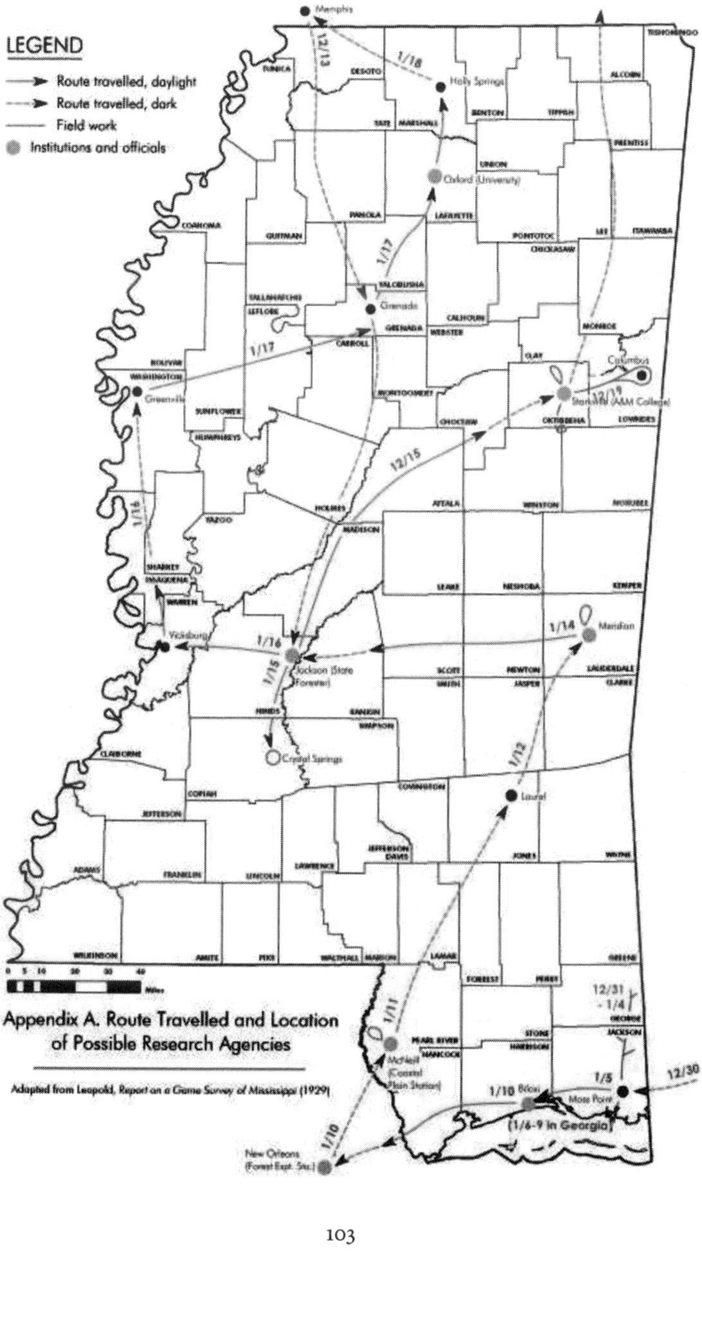

Appendix A. Route Travelled and Location of Possible Research Agencies

Adapted from Leopold, *Report on a Game Survey of Mississippi* (1929)

Appendix 4

Fannye Cook letter to Aldo Leopold, January 28, 1929

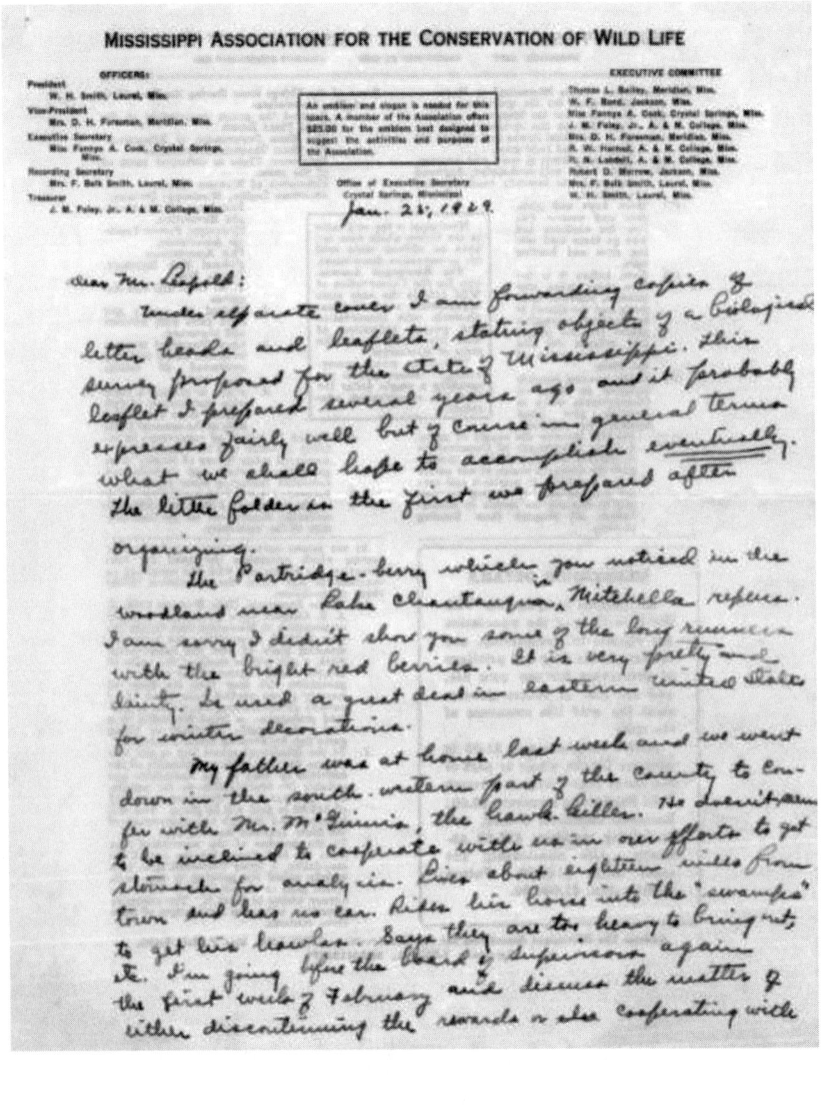

MISSISSIPPI ASSOCIATION FOR THE CONSERVATION OF WILD LIFE

OFFICERS:

President
W. H. Smith, Laurel, Miss.

Vice-President
Mrs. D. H. Foreman, Meridian, Miss.

Executive Secretary
Miss Fannye A. Cook, Crystal Springs, Miss.

Recording Secretary
Mrs. F. Belk Smith, Laurel, Miss.

Treasurer
J. M. Foley, Jr., A. & M. College, Miss.

An emblem and slogan is needed for this ... A member of the Association offers $25.00 for the emblem best designed to suggest the activities and purposes of the Association.

EXECUTIVE COMMITTEE

Thomas L. Bailey, Meridian, Miss.
W. F. Bond, Jackson, Miss.
Miss Fannye A. Cook, Crystal Springs, Miss.
J. M. Foley, Jr., A. & M. College, Miss.
Mrs. D. H. Foreman, Meridian, Miss.
R. W. Harned, A. & M. College, Miss.
R. N. Lobdell, A. & M. College, Miss.
Robert D. Morrow, Jackson, Miss.
Mrs. F. Belk Smith, Laurel, Miss.
W. H. Smith, Laurel, Miss.

Office of Executive Secretary
Crystal Springs, Mississippi

Jan. 28, 1929.

Dear Mr. Leopold:

Under separate cover I am forwarding copies of
letter heads and leaflets, stating objects of a biological
survey proposed for the State of Mississippi. This
leaflet I prepared several years ago and it probably
expresses fairly well but of course in general terms
what we shall hope to accomplish eventually.
The little folder is the first we prepared after
organizing.

The Partridge-berry which you noticed in the
woodland near Lake Chautauqua is Mitchella repens.
I am sorry I didn't show you some of the long runners
with the bright red berries. It is very pretty and
dainty. Is used a great deal in eastern United States
for winter decorations.

My father was at home last week and we went
down in the south-western part of the County to con-
fer with Mr. McGinnis, the hawk-killer. He doesn't seem
to be inclined to cooperate with us in our efforts to get
stomachs for analysis. Lives about eighteen miles from
town and has no car. Rides his horse into the "swamps"
to get his hawks. Says they are too heavy to bring out,
etc. I'm going before the board of supervisors again
the first week of February and discuss the matter of
either discontinuing the rewards or else cooperating with

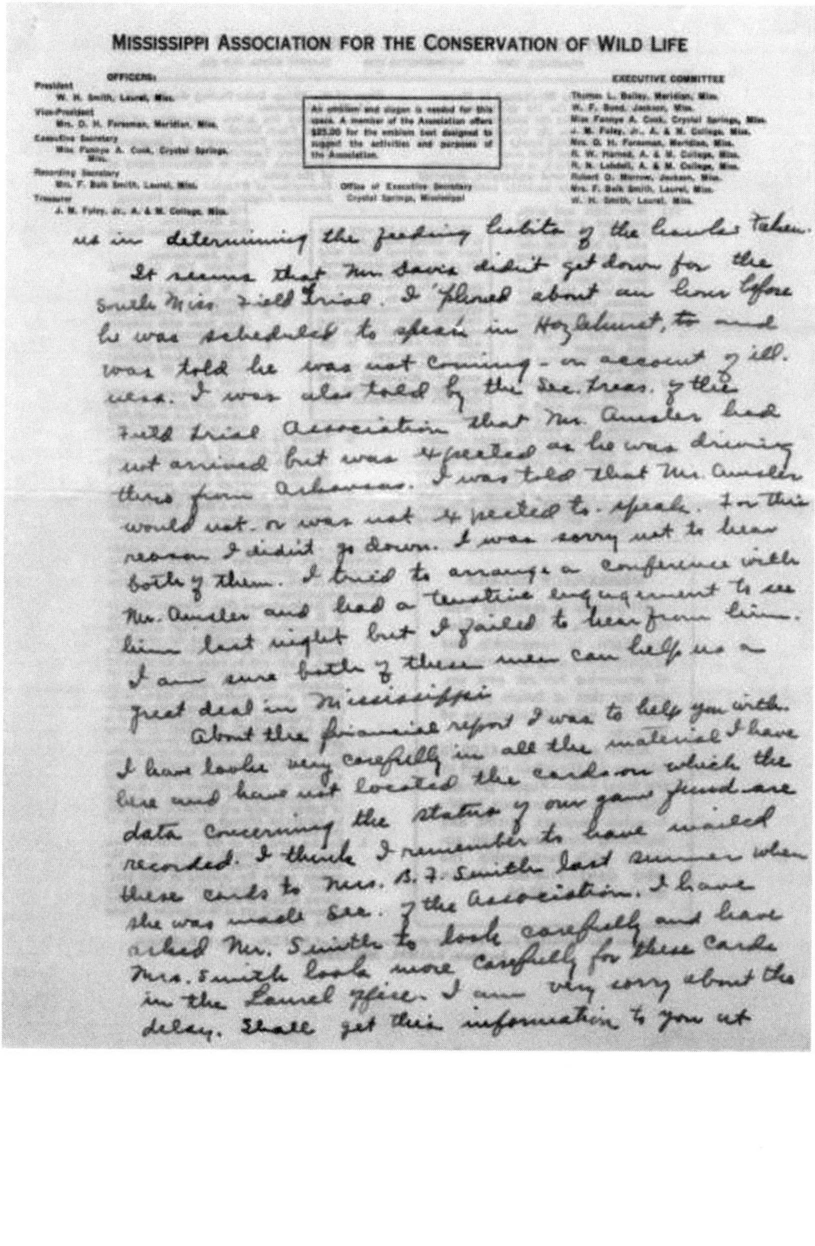

MISSISSIPPI ASSOCIATION FOR THE CONSERVATION OF WILD LIFE

OFFICERS:
President
W. H. Smith, Laurel, Miss.
Vice-President
Mrs. D. H. Foreman, Meridian, Miss.
Executive Secretary
Miss Fannye A. Cook, Crystal Springs, Miss.
Recording Secretary
Mrs. F. Balk Smith, Laurel, Miss.
Treasurer
J. M. Foley, Jr., A. & M. College, Miss.

An emblem and slogan is needed for this space. A member of the Association offers $25.00 for the emblem best designed to suggest the activities and purposes of the Association.

Office of Executive Secretary
Crystal Springs, Mississippi

EXECUTIVE COMMITTEE
Thomas L. Bailey, Meridian, Miss.
W. F. Bond, Jackson, Miss.
Miss Fannye A. Cook, Crystal Springs, Miss.
J. M. Foley, Jr., A. & M. College, Miss.
Mrs. D. H. Foreman, Meridian, Miss.
R. W. Harned, A. & M. College, Miss.
R. N. Lobdell, A. & M. College, Miss.
Robert D. Morrow, Jackson, Miss.
Mrs. F. Balk Smith, Laurel, Miss.
W. H. Smith, Laurel, Miss.

us in determining the feeding habits of the hawks taken.

It seems that Mr. Davis didn't get down for the South Miss. Field Trial. I 'phoned about an hour before he was scheduled to speak in Hazlehurst, to and was told he was not coming - on account of illness. I was also told by the Sec. treas. of the Field Trial Association that Mr. Ansler had not arrived but was expected as he was driving there from Arkansas. I was told that Mr. Ansler would not - or was not expected to - speak. For this reason I didn't go down. I was sorry not to hear both of them. I tried to arrange a conference with Mr. Ansler and had a tentative engagement to see him last night but I failed to hear from him. I am sure both of these men can help us a great deal in Mississippi

About the financial report I was to help you with. I have looked very carefully in all the material I have here and have not located the cards on which the data concerning the status of our game fund are recorded. I think I remember to have mailed these cards to Mrs. B. F. Smith last summer when she was made Sec. of the Association. I have asked Mr. Smith to look carefully and have Mrs. Smith look more carefully for these cards in the Laurel office. I am very sorry about the delay. Shall get this information to you at

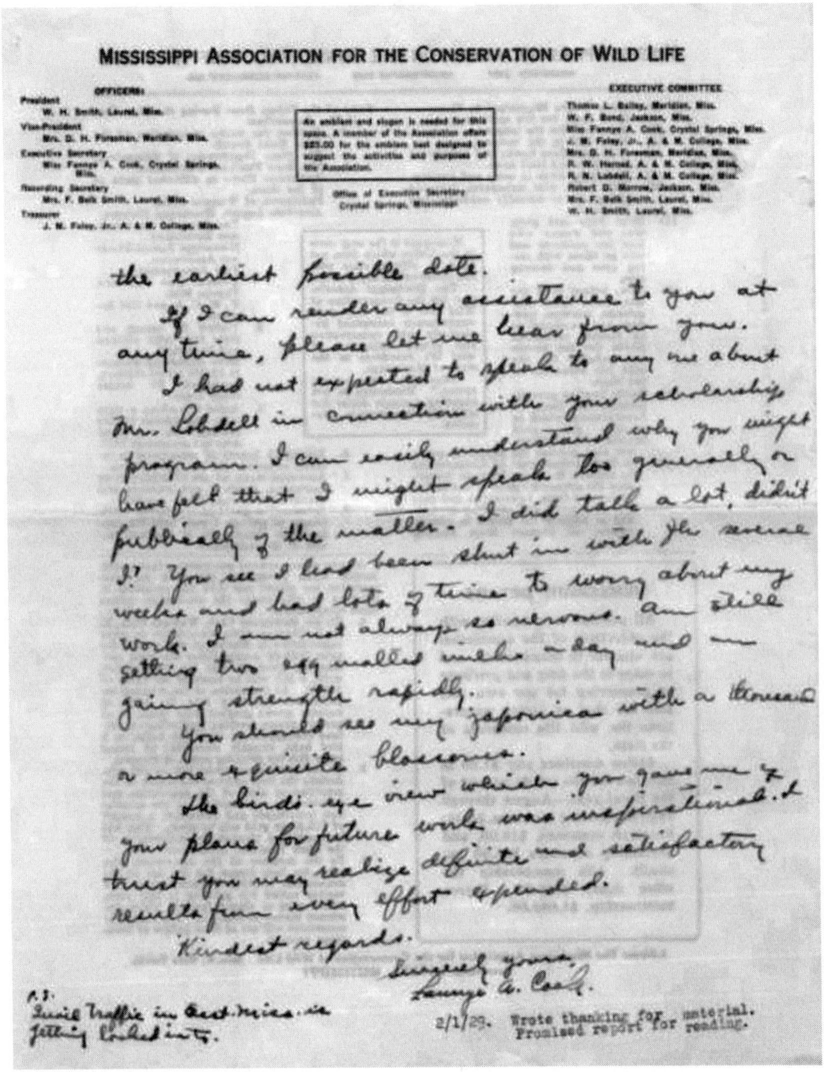

MISSISSIPPI ASSOCIATION FOR THE CONSERVATION OF WILD LIFE

OFFICERS:
President
W. H. Smith, Laurel, Miss.
Vice-President
Mrs. D. H. Foreman, Meridian, Miss.
Executive Secretary
Miss Fannye A. Cook, Crystal Springs, Miss.
Recording Secretary
Mrs. F. Belk Smith, Laurel, Miss.
Treasurer
J. M. Foley, Jr., A. & M. College, Miss.

An emblem and slogan is needed for this space. A member of the Association offers $25.00 for the emblem best designed to suggest the activities and purposes of the Association.

Office of Executive Secretary
Crystal Springs, Mississippi

EXECUTIVE COMMITTEE
Thomas L. Bailey, Meridian, Miss.
W. F. Bond, Jackson, Miss.
Miss Fannye A. Cook, Crystal Springs, Miss.
J. M. Foley, Jr., A. & M. College, Miss.
Mrs. D. H. Foreman, Meridian, Miss.
R. W. Harned, A. & M. College, Miss.
R. N. Lobdell, A. & M. College, Miss.
Robert D. Morrow, Jackson, Miss.
Mrs. F. Belk Smith, Laurel, Miss.
W. H. Smith, Laurel, Miss.

the earliest possible date.
If I can render any assistance to you at
any time, please let me hear from you.
I had not expected to speak to any one about
Mr. Lobdell in connection with your scholarship
program. I can easily understand why you might
have felt that I might speak too generally or
publically of the matter. I did talk a lot, didn't
I? You see I had been shut in with the several
weeks and had lots of time to worry about my
work. I am not always so nervous. Am still
getting two egg malted milks a day and am
gaining strength rapidly.
You should see my japonica with a thousand
or more exquisite blossoms.
The birds-eye view which you gave me of
your plans for future work was inspirational. I
trust you may realize definite and satisfactory
results from every effort expended.
Kindest regards.
Sincerely yours,
Fannye A. Cook.

P.S.
Quail Traffic in East. Miss. is
getting looked into.

2/1/29. Wrote thanking for material.
Promised report for reading.

Appendix 5

Fannye Cook letter to Aldo Leopold, March 14, 1929

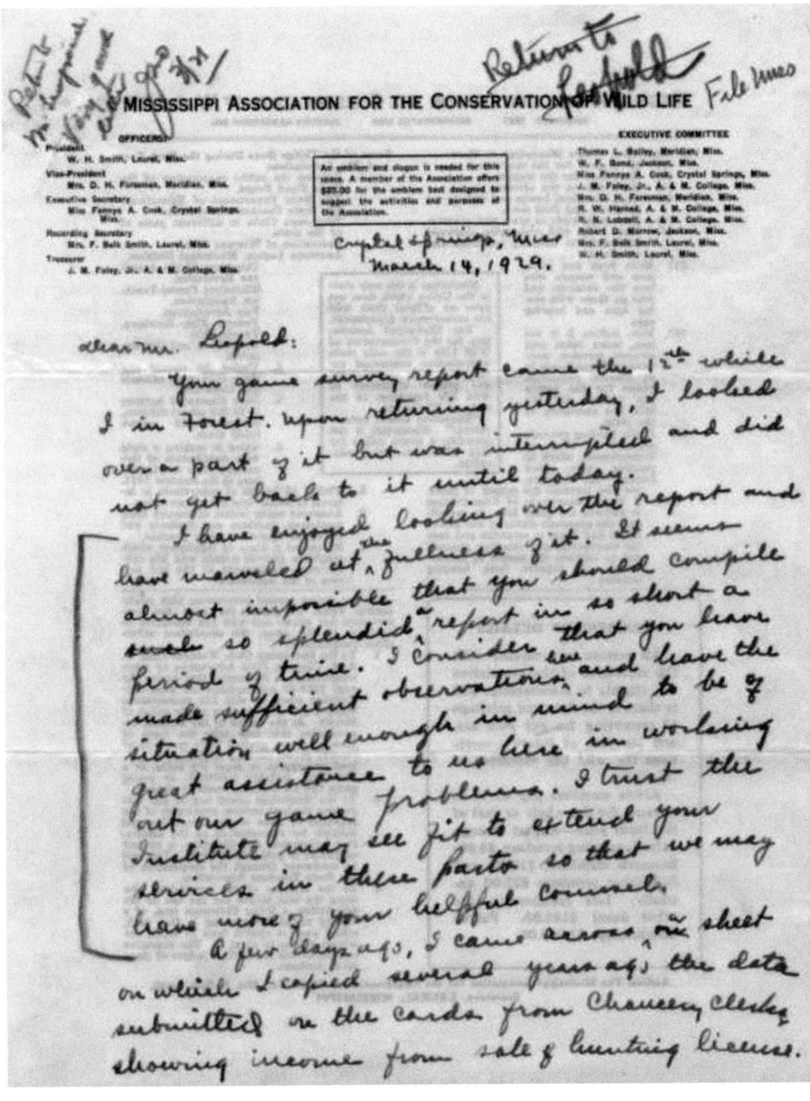

Return to Leopold

File mss

MISSISSIPPI ASSOCIATION FOR THE CONSERVATION OF WILD LIFE

OFFICERS

President
W. H. Smith, Laurel, Miss.

Vice-President
Mrs. D. H. Foreman, Meridian, Miss.

Executive Secretary
Miss Fannye A. Cook, Crystal Springs, Miss.

Recording Secretary
Mrs. F. Belk Smith, Laurel, Miss.

Treasurer
J. M. Foley, Jr., A. & M. College, Miss.

An emblem and slogan is needed for this space. A member of the Association offers $25.00 for the emblem best designed to suggest the activities and purposes of the Association.

EXECUTIVE COMMITTEE

Thomas L. Bailey, Meridian, Miss.
W. F. Bond, Jackson, Miss.
Miss Fannye A. Cook, Crystal Springs, Miss.
J. M. Foley, Jr., A. & M. College, Miss.
Mrs. D. H. Foreman, Meridian, Miss.
R. W. Harned, A. & M. College, Miss.
R. N. Lobdell, A. & M. College, Miss.
Robert D. Morrow, Jackson, Miss.
Mrs. F. Belk Smith, Laurel, Miss.
W. H. Smith, Laurel, Miss.

Crystal Springs, Miss.
March 14, 1929.

Dear Mr. Leopold:

Your game survey report came the 12th while I in Forest. Upon returning yesterday, I looked over a part of it but was interrupted and did not get back to it until today.

I have enjoyed looking over the report and have marveled at the fullness of it. It seems almost impossible that you should compile such a splendid report in so short a period of time. I consider that you have made sufficient observations and have the situation well enough in mind to be of great assistance to us here in working out our game problems. I trust the Institute may see fit to extend your services in these parts so that we may have more of your helpful counsel.

A few days ago, I came across a sheet on which I copied several years ago the data submitted on the cards from Chancery Clerks showing income from sale of hunting license.

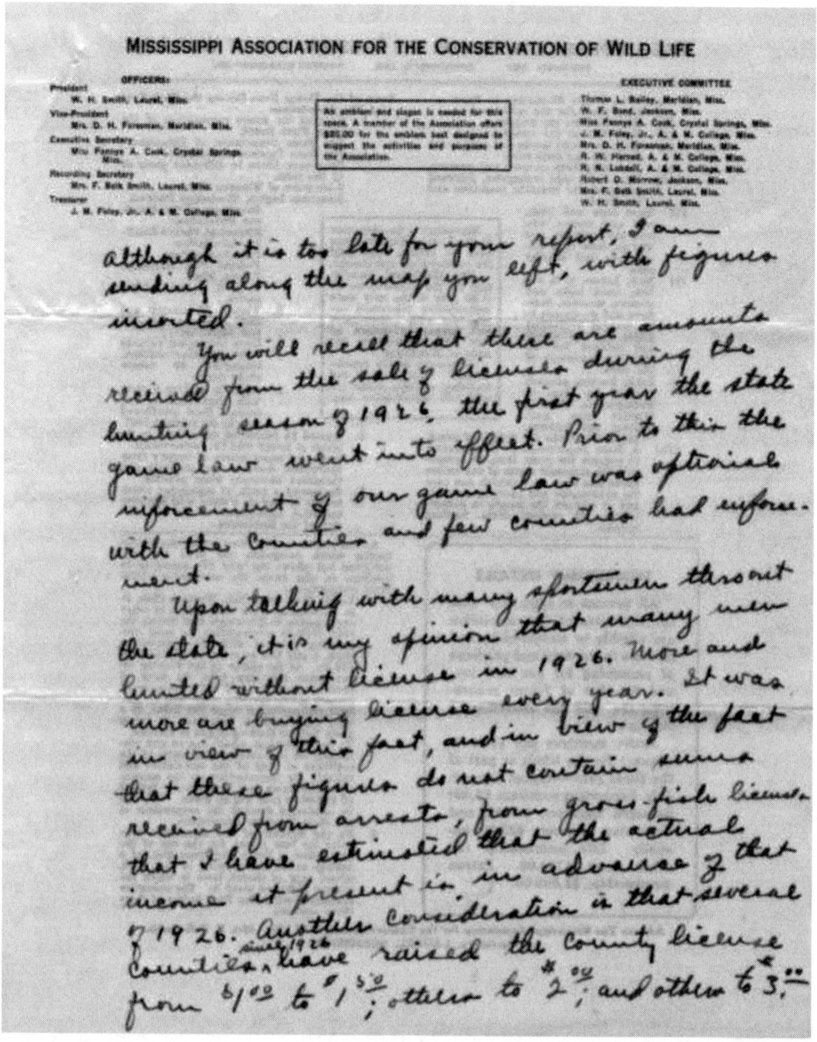

MISSISSIPPI ASSOCIATION FOR THE CONSERVATION OF WILD LIFE

OFFICERS:
President
W. H. Smith, Laurel, Miss.
Vice-President
Mrs. D. H. Foreman, Meridian, Miss.
Executive Secretary
Miss Fannye A. Cook, Crystal Springs, Miss.
Recording Secretary
Mrs. F. Bek Smith, Laurel, Miss.
Treasurer
J. M. Foley, Jr., A. & M. College, Miss.

An emblem and slogan is needed for this space. A member of the Association offers $20.00 for the emblem best designed to suggest the activities and purposes of the Association.

EXECUTIVE COMMITTEE
Thomas L. Bailey, Meridian, Miss.
W. F. Bond, Jackson, Miss.
Miss Fannye A. Cook, Crystal Springs, Miss.
J. M. Foley, Jr., A. & M. College, Miss.
Mrs. D. H. Foreman, Meridian, Miss.
R. W. Harned, A. & M. College, Miss.
R. N. Lobdell, A. & M. College, Miss.
Robert D. Morrow, Jackson, Miss.
Mrs. F. Bek Smith, Laurel, Miss.
W. H. Smith, Laurel, Miss.

although it is too late for your report, I am sending along the map you left, with figures inserted.

You will recall that there are amounts received from the sale of licenses during the hunting season of 1926, the first year the state game law went into effect. Prior to this the enforcement of our game law was optional with the counties and few counties had enforcement.

Upon talking with many sportsmen thruout the state, it is my opinion that many men hunted without license in 1926. More and more are buying license every year. It was in view of this fact, and in view of the fact that these figures do not contain sums received from arrests, from gross-fish license that I have estimated that the actual income at present is in advance of that of 1926. Another consideration is that several counties, since 1926, have raised the county license from $1.00 to $1.50; others to $2.00; and others to $3.00

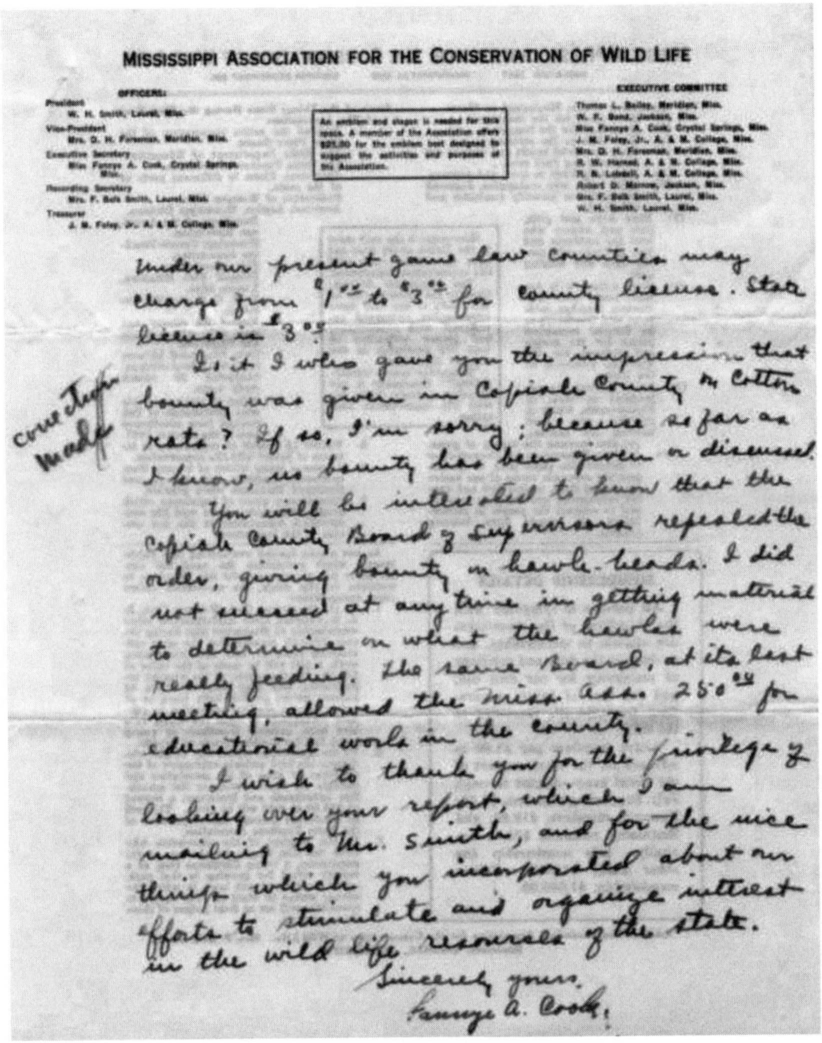

MISSISSIPPI ASSOCIATION FOR THE CONSERVATION OF WILD LIFE

OFFICERS:
President
W. H. Smith, Laurel, Miss.
Vice-President
Mrs. D. H. Foreman, Meridian, Miss.
Executive Secretary
Miss Fannye A. Cook, Crystal Springs, Miss.
Recording Secretary
Mrs. F. Bob Smith, Laurel, Miss.
Treasurer
J. M. Foley, Jr., A. & M. College, Miss.

An emblem and slogan is needed for this space. A member of the Association offers $25.00 for the emblem best designed to suggest the activities and purposes of this Association.

EXECUTIVE COMMITTEE
Thomas L. Bailey, Meridian, Miss.
W. F. Bond, Jackson, Miss.
Miss Fannye A. Cook, Crystal Springs, Miss.
J. M. Foley, Jr., A. & M. College, Miss.
Mrs. D. H. Foreman, Meridian, Miss.
R. W. Harned, A. & M. College, Miss.
R. B. Lobdell, A. & M. College, Miss.
Robert D. Morrow, Jackson, Miss.
Mrs. F. Bob Smith, Laurel, Miss.
W. H. Smith, Laurel, Miss.

Under our present game law counties may charge from $1.00 to $3.00 for county license. State license is $3.00.

Is it I who gave you the impression that bounty was given in Copiah County on cotton rats? If so, I'm sorry; because so far as I know, no bounty has been given or discussed.

correction made

You will be interested to know that the Copiah County Board of Supervisors repealed the order, giving bounty on hawk-heads. I did not succeed at any time in getting material to determine on what the hawks were really feeding. The same Board, at its last meeting, allowed the Miss. Ass. 25.00 for educational work in the county.

I wish to thank you for the privilege of looking over your report, which I am mailing to Mr. Smith, and for the nice things which you incorporated about our efforts to stimulate and organize interest in the wild life resources of the state.

Sincerely yours,

Fannye A. Cook.

Appendix 6

Aldo Leopold letter to Fannye Cook, March 19, 1929

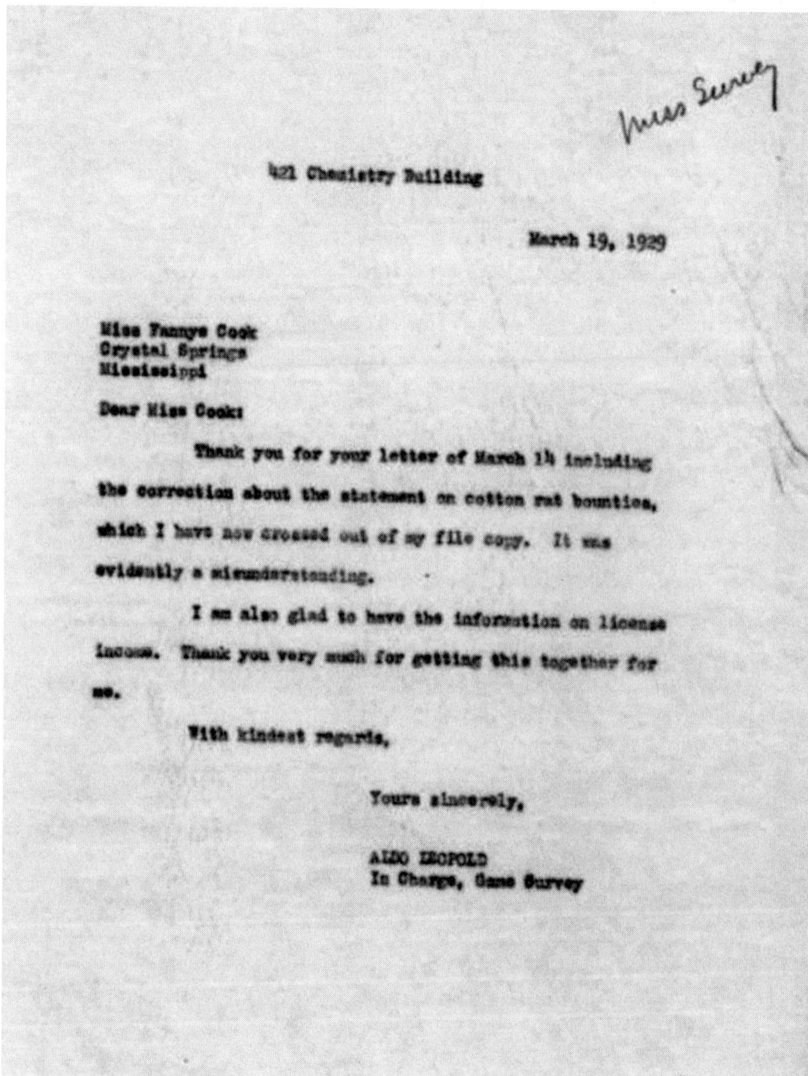

421 Chemistry Building

March 19, 1929

Miss Fannye Cook
Crystal Springs
Mississippi

Dear Miss Cook:

Thank you for your letter of March 14 including the correction about the statement on cotton rat bounties, which I have now crossed out of my file copy. It was evidently a misunderstanding.

I am also glad to have the information on license income. Thank you very much for getting this together for me.

With kindest regards,

Yours sincerely,

ALDO LEOPOLD
In Charge, Game Survey

Appendix 7

Fannye Cook letter to University of Washington, June 20, 1952

Miss.

GAME AND FISH COMMISSION

STATE OF MISSISSIPPI

COMMISSIONERS
H. C. KINSEY, TUPELO
CHAIRMAN
OLLIE L. OTT, FOREST
VICE-CHAIRMAN
DOUGLAS WRIGHT, JR.
VICKSBURG, SECRETARY

COMMISSIONERS
P. K. McLAIN, MONTICELLO
DR. W. E. JOHNSON, RIPLEY
GEORGE T. DAVIS, BENOIT
H. BEE WOOD, MCCOMB
J. W. SEALE, CALHOUN CITY

JACKSON, MISSISSIPPI

R. M. FREEMAN
DIRECTOR OF CONSERVATION

May 20, 1952

P. O. BOX 451
PHONE 2-9361

Mr. Joseph J. Hickey, Asso. Professor
College of Agriculture
Depart. of Wildlife Management
University of Wisconsin
Madison, 6, Wisconsin

Dear Mr. Hickey:

On behalf of the Mississippi State Game and Fish Commission I wish to acknowledge the receipt of the "Report on a Game Survey of Mississippi" by Aldo Leopold and to thank you for your kindness in sending it.

This very interesting report, beautifully bound, is a fine addition to our library. It contains information of great interest to those of us engaged in game surveys in this state.

We are very grateful to you for this contribution.

Sincerely yours,

Fannye A. Cook

Fannye A. Cook
Museum Curator

FAC:aj

"Develop and Conserve Mississippi's Game and Fish Resources"

THIS DEPARTMENT OPERATES WITHOUT ANY APPROPRIATION FROM THE STATE

Appendix 8

On the Science of Fannye A. Cook

A scholar of human history will peruse the writings available in a library to develop an understanding of events in the past and draw connections among events through time. A natural historian will employ biological collections housed in museums around the world in much the same way. A cursory inspection of any properly archived specimen will reveal a bevy of facts including the classification of the specimen, its location of capture, when it was captured, and who did the capturing.

The intrepid researcher will delve further, examining the specimen to discover information about its life in that time and place. He or she can extract answers to many questions regarding its constitution, whether or not it was actively breeding, what it was eating, and even whether the specimen was parasitized or shows signs of being fed upon by larger consumers. Expanding one's investigation to the specimen housed nearby, and the one next to that, will open the possibility to draw connections between organisms in space and time. Understanding the past allows for a more informed appraisal of current observations, made all the more important in times of rapid environmental change brought about through human activities and natural events.

It was for the purpose of providing this insight to the state of Mississippi's natural resource managers, to the public that utilizes its natural resources, and to the legislators that govern their use, that Fannye A. Cook founded the biological collections housed at the Mississippi Museum of Natural Science (MMNS). Miss Cook served as the first director of the museum, known then as the State Wildlife Museum, beginning in 1933 and until her retirement in 1958. Although she did serve in an administrative capacity, Miss Cook was also the museum's first research scientist, curator, educator, and displays artist. Her varied responsibilities ultimately resulted in the multi-tiered, but very much interrelated, mission and structure of the MMNS today.

Miss Cook directed the first statewide floral and faunal survey as part of the Works Progress Administration (WPA) between 1936 and 1941. The majority of specimens within the museum's biological collections during her tenure had their origins in this massive and historic effort, although there are a small number dating back to the nineteenth century. The WPA survey resulted in a total of ninety-eight hundred cataloged species lots of fishes, amphibians, and reptiles. The distributions of Mississippi plants and animals described during this survey are employed to the present day by the Mississippi Department of Wildlife, Fisheries, and Parks as a reference for gauging species range expansions and declines when new survey data become available.

Not one to simply let these specimens sit on the shelves, Miss Cook embodied the intrepid researcher, putting the information provided into practical use. Specimens were sent to classrooms throughout Mississippi, giving students a chance to study up close animals that they might otherwise only see from a distance. She also made careful note of the physical characteristics of these specimens, culminating in treatises on Mississippi's snakes, salamanders, and fishes, published in 1954, 1957, and 1959, respectively.

Miss Cook's best known published work, *Freshwater Fishes in Mississippi*, would not have been possible without the opportunity to thoroughly examine preserved fish specimens available in the biological collections. Approximately six thousand fish specimens representing 125 species were examined. These specimens were derived from a total of 245 survey locations encompassing every major river system in Mississippi.

Miss Cook employed counts of scales, counts of fin support structures, careful measures of distances between external features, and internal anatomy to develop the first "dichotomous key" to Mississippi fishes. A dichotomous key presents the user with a series of paired statements referring to alternative characteristics that may be present on an organism in need of identification. By eliminating organisms with characteristics that do not represent the organism in question, the user is eventually brought to the correct identification. Miss Cook's key served as the principal identification tool in fish biology classrooms and laboratories throughout Mississippi for decades and was seminal to modern editions.

Upon examination of her science, a pattern emerges. Miss Cook's was a pattern of data collection, data analysis, and dissemination of the garnered information to various user groups. This is embedded in the mission statement of the MMNS today:

> The mission of the Mississippi Museum of Natural Science is to promote understanding and appreciation of Mississippi's biological diversity through collections, research, scientific databases, education, and exhibits; and to inspire the people of our state to respect the environment and to preserve natural Mississippi.

Presently, more than one million specimens in the biological collections are cared for, and studied by, research biologists and curators employed in the MMNS Research Division. The MMNS Heritage Division works in conjunction with the researchers to apply the garnered information to the state of Mississippi's ever-evolving conservation strategy. It is also via this collaboration that results are conveyed to other government agencies, legislators, and the scientific community. The MMNS Education, Exhibits, and Aquariums Divisions are charged with taking the information generated by the Research and Heritage Divisions, as well as from many other sources, and making it available to the benefit of the general public through educator training programs, student activities, and engaging displays that ignite wonder.

A study of Fannye Cook's daily work life can be made at one particular display in which her office has been painstakingly recreated. The viewer will find there the implements fundamental to her many duties: measuring devices, taxidermy tools, specimen mounts and drawers, drawings for her key to fishes, a typewriter, a teacher's guidebook, and others. A study of her scientific ethos can be made by examination of the structure and function of the institution she played a crucial role in founding.

Matt E. Roberts
Research Program Coordinator
Mississippi Museum of Natural Science
Jackson, Mississippi
16 December 2016

Notes

One. Girlhood in Crystal Springs, 1889–1907

1. Eudora Welty to John Robinson, 28 March 1944, Eudora Welty Collection, Mississippi Department of Archives and History (MDAH), Jackson.

2. Fannye Cook, handwritten note, Cabinet 1, Archive Collection, Mississippi Museum of Natural Science (MMNS), Jackson.

3. William Souder, "Angry Bird," *Smithsonian*, September 2014, 64–65. This article was written on the one hundredth anniversary of the death of Martha, the last passenger pigeon known on earth.

4. Ibid., 64.

5. Dorothy Moore Alford, *Reflections and Recognitions: Crystal Springs, Mississippi, 1820–1972*, published by author, n.d., 148.

6. Cook family genealogical charts, MMNS.

7. William Bizzell, interview by author, 20 March 2011.

8. Ibid.

9. Alford, *Reflections and Recognitions*, 2.

10. T. P. Lockwood, "Reminiscences of Old Crystal Springs," *Crystal Springs' Centennial Celebration, 1858–1958* (Crystal Springs: Meteor, 1958), 3.

11. Alford, *Reflections and Recognitions*, 3.

12. Ibid.

13. Ibid., 47.

14. Lockwood, "Reminiscences," 2.

15. Alford, *Reflections and Recognitions*, 48.

16. Ibid.

17. Ibid., 6.

18. G. M. Cook to Fannye Cook, 30 March 1926, Fannye Cook papers, MMNS.

19. Alford, *Reflections and Recognitions*, 12.

20. Ibid., 10.

21. Ibid., 13.

22. Ibid., 14.

23. William Bizzell, interview by author, 26 June 2011.

24. Rita Bizzell, interview by author, 2 June 2011.

25. Edwin J. Becker, "Ladies Afield," *Independent Woman,* April 1946.

26. "Darwin in the House," *Smithsonian*, February 2013, 60–67.

27. Ibid., 67.

28. Ken Burns, *The Roosevelts*, Public Broadcasting Service, Sept. 2014. DVD.

29. Minor Ferris Buchanan, *Holt Collier: His Life, His Roosevelt Hunts, and The Origin of the Teddy Bear* (Jackson: Centennial Press, 2002).

30. Alford, *Reflections and Recognitions*, 65.

31. "Application for Position of Teacher," The Panama Canal, Division of Schools, 16 July 1915, National Personnel Records Center, Saint Louis.

32. Alford, *Reflections and Recognitions*, 67.

Two. Columbus to College, 1907–11

1. *Industrial Institute and College Catalog, 1911–12* (Columbus, MS: Industrial Institute and College, 1911), 85.

2. Bridget Smith Pieschel and Stephen Robert Pieschel, *Loyal Daughters: One Hundred Years at Mississippi University for Women, 1884–1994* (Jackson: University Press of Mississippi, 1994), 6.

3. Ibid., 61.

4. *Industrial Institute and College Catalog, 1911–1912.*

5. Pieschel and Pieschel, *Loyal Daughters*, 190.

6. *Industrial Institute and College Catalog, 1911–1912.*

7. Pieschel and Pieschel, *Loyal Daughters*, 67.

8. Ibid., 61.

9. *Industrial Institute and College Catalog, 1911–1912*, 50.

10. Ibid.

11. Pieschel and Pieschel, *Loyal Daughters*, 176.

12. Ibid., 65–66.

13. Ibid., 61.

14. Ibid., 63.

15. Ibid., 162.

16. David Carson, "Elizabeth Lee Hazen," in *Mississippi Women: Their Histories, Their Lives*, vol. 1, ed. Martha Swain, Elizabeth Payne, and Marjorie Spruill (Athens: University of Georgia Press, 2003), 131.

17. Pieschel and Pieschel, *Loyal Daughters*, 57.

18. Marcie Sanders, Papers, Mississippi University for Women Archives, Columbus, Mississippi.

19. "Application for Position of Teacher."

20. *Meh Lady* (Columbus, MS: Industrial Institute and College, 1911–12), 16.

Three. School Principal, Teacher, and Student, 1911–18

1. Suzanne Marrs, "En Route to a Curtain of Green," in Swain et al., *Mississippi Women*, 181.

2. "Application for Position of Teacher."

3. Rita Bizzell, interview by author, 26 July 2010.

4. William Bizzell, interview by author, 16 November 2012.

5. "Application for Position of Teacher."

6. Katherine M. Cook, *Public Education in the Panama Canal Zone*. US Department of the Interior, Office of Education, Bulletin 139, No. 8, 17.

7. Ibid., 21–22.

8. Ibid., 47.

9. Ibid., 16–17.

10. Ibid., 17.

11. Cook family genealogical charts, MMNS.

12. Panama Canal documents, National Personnel Records Center, Saint Louis.

13. *Crystal Springs' Centennial Celebration: 1858–1958* (Crystal Springs: Meteor, 1958), 10.

14. Dorothy Shawhan, "Minnie Brewer," in Swain et al., *Mississippi Women*, 164.

15. Martha Swain, *Ellen S. Woodward: New Deal Advocate for Women* (Jackson: University Press of Mississippi, 1995), 7.

16. Dorothy S. Shawhan and Martha H. Swain, *Lucy Somerville Howorth: New Deal Lawyer, Politician, and Feminist from the South* (Baton Rouge: Louisiana State University Press, 2006), 20.

17. Wyoming Department of Education, *Wyoming Education Directory, 1917–18* (Cheyenne: Wyoming Department of Education, 1917).

18. "Snap Shots at Home News," *Ladner Wyoming State Journal*, 25 July 1919, 1.

19. Eudora Welty to Mary Margaret Millar, 5 December 1971, Eudora Welty Collection, MDAH.

Four. The Washington Years, 1918–26

1. Treasury Department documents, National Personnel Records Center, Saint Louis.

2. Wiley Pruitt, "The Best of All Breathing: Hunting and Environmental Change in Mississippi, 1900–1980" (master's thesis, University of Mississippi, December 1991).

3. Anne Firor Scott and Andrew MacKay Scott, *One Half the People: The Fight for Woman Suffrage* (Urbana: University of Illinois Press, 1982).

4. Anne Firor Scott, "Nellie Nugent Somerville," in *Notable American Women: The Modern Period*, ed. Barbara Sicherman and Carol Hurd Green (Cambridge, Mass: Belknap Press, 1980), 254–56.

5. Calvin Woodward, "IRS Seems Past its Glory Days," *Jackson Clarion Ledger*, 2 June 2013.

6. Treasury Department documents, National Personnel Records Center, Saint Louis.

7. Martha Ellen Pierce Cook to Fannye Cook, 21 September 1919, Family Letters, MMNS.

8. *University Bulletin* (Washington, DC: George Washington University, 1923–24).

9. Paul Bartsch, "Notes on the Heron of the District of Columbia," *Smithsonian* 45 (1903): 104–11.

10. S. Dillon Ripley and James A. Steed, *Alexander Wetmore, 1886–1978: A Biographical Memoir* (Washington, DC: National Academy of Sciences, 1978).

11. Treasury Department documents, National Personnel Records Center, Saint Louis.

12. Bird Catalog, MMNS.

13. Collection documents, Smithsonian National Museum of Natural History, Washington, DC.

14. *General Laws of Mississippi*, (Meridian, Miss.: Interstate Printers, 1926), 178, 280.

15. William H. Turcotte and David L. Watts, *Birds of Mississippi* (Jackson: University Press of Mississippi: 1999), 8.

Five. Bringing the Fight Back Home, 1926–32

1. John Muir, "The Scenic Route," *Mental Floss*, July–Aug. 2013, 46–47.

2. "Brave Thinkers," *The Atlantic*, November 2012, 78.

3. Turcotte and Watts, *Birds of Mississippi*, 16.

4. Mary Hamilton, *Trials of the Earth* (Jackson: University Press of Mississippi, 1992), xii.

5. Fran Holman Johnson, "*The Gift of the Wild Things*": *The Life of Caroline Dormon* (Lafayette: University of Southwestern Louisiana, 1990).

6. Ibid., 38.

7. B. E. Gandy, "In Memoriam: Miss Fannye A. Cook," *The Mississippi Kite* 1, no. 1 (May 1965): 8–10.

8. Ripley and Steed, *Alexander Wetmore*. Cook came to know Dr. Wetmore at the Smithsonian. He was born in Wisconsin and was three years older than Cook. Like Cook he became interested in birds as a child of five years when his mother gave him Chapman's *Handbook of Birds in Eastern North America*.

9. Cook to Bartsch, 4 August 1926, Folder Cook, Fannye, Box 8, Collection no. 73, Smithsonian Institution Archives, Washington, DC.

10. Ibid., 7 June 1927.

11. Ibid., 1 Oct. 1927.

12. Ibid.

13. W. H. Turcotte, "MMNS Celebrates First Fifty Years," *MMNS Newsletter* 2, no. 1 (1983).

14. Fannye Cook, "Prospectus of the Mississippi Association for the Conservation of Wild Life," in Aldo Leopold, *Report on a Game Survey of Mississippi* (1929; repr. with maps and correspondence, Jackson: Mississippi Museum of Natural Science, 2010), 80.

15. Flyer, Mississippi Association for the Conservation of Wild Life, 1928, quoted in Libby Hartfield and Alan Huffman, "Fannye A. Cook, Pioneer Conservationist and Scientist, 1889–1964," *Mississippi History Now* (June 2009), http://www.mshistorynow.mdah.ms.gov/articles/313/fannye-cook-pioneer-conservationist.

16. Dennis Mitchell, *A New History of Mississippi* (Jackson: University Press of Mississippi, 2014), 338.

17. "Frances A. Cook, Pioneer Conservationist and Scientist, 1889–1964," typewritten document, MMNS.

18. Turcotte and Watts, *Birds of Mississippi*, 9.

19. Shawhan and Swain, *Lucy Somerville Howorth*, 70.

20. Aldo Leopold, *Report on a Game Survey of Mississippi* (1929; repr. with maps and correspondence, Jackson: Mississippi Museum of Natural Science, 2010). See appendixes 2–7.

21. Ibid., 106.

22. Leopold to Cook, 6 January 1928, Leopold letters, MMNS.

23. Cook to Leopold, 28 January 1929, in Leopold, *Report*, 91–93.

24. Cook to Leopold, 14 March 1929, in Leopold, *Report*, 100–102.

25. Leopold to Cook, 27 December 1929, Leopold letters, MMNS.

26. Editor and compiler was Mary P. Stevens, Librarian for MMNS.

27. Fannye Cook, "Annual Report of Executive Secretary," Mississippi Association for the Conservation of Wild Life, 14 July 1928, MMNS.

28. Ibid.

29. Fannye Cook, "Annual Report of Executive Secretary," Mississippi Association for the Conservation of Wild Life, 19 July 1929, MMNS.

30. "Woman Nature Student Sees Success as Near," *Jackson Daily News*, 4 August 1929, 6–7.

31. Dyana Z. Furmansky, *Rosalie Edge: Hawk of Mercy* (Athens, GA: University of Georgia Press, 2009), 114, 235.

32. Ibid., 138.

33. Ibid., 175.

34. Becker, "Ladies Afield," 106–108.

35. Pruitt, "Best of All Breathing."

36. John Turcotte, email message to author, 15 October 2010.

37. W. H. Turcotte, "MMNS Celebrates."

38. Cook to Bartsch, 11 March 1931, Smithsonian Institution Archives.

39. Shawhan and Swain, *Lucy Somerville Howorth*, 70.

40. *Jackson Daily News*, 17 January 1932.

41. Shawhan and Swain, *Lucy Somerville Howorth*, 70.

42. Ibid., 69. On July 1, 1989, the State Parks Department merged with the Mississippi Department of Wildlife Conservation (MDWC) to become Mississippi Department of Wildlife, Fisheries, and Parks. MDWC was formed from the Mississippi Game and Fish Commission.

43. C. E. Lilly to Fannye Cook, 8 February 1932, Fannye Cook papers, MMNS.

44. Fannye Cook to C. E. Lilly, 16 February 1932, Fannye Cook papers, MMNS.

45. Cook family genealogical charts, MMNS.

46. Fannye Cook papers, MMNS.

47. Mississippi House of Representatives, *Journal of the House of Representatives of the State of Mississippi* (Jackson: Hederman Brothers, 1932), 342.

48. Mississippi Senate, *Journal of the Senate of the State of Mississippi* (Jackson: Hederman Brothers, 1932), 405.

49. Mitchell, *New History*, 338.

50. Cook to Bartsch, 23 Mar. 1932, Smithsonian Institution Archives.

51. Bartsch to Cook, 9 April 1932, Fannye Cook papers, MMNS.

52. W. H. Turcotte, "MMNS Celebrates First 50 Years," *Mississippi Museum of Natural Science Newsletter* 2, no. 1, 1983.

53. Fannye Cook, press release with handwritten note, Smithsonian Institution Archives.

Six. The Great Depression and the WPA, 1934–41

1. Joe Howorth to W. E. McIntyre, 25 January 1936, MMNS.

2. Ibid.

3. Lonnie Williamson, *Restoring America's Wildlife, 1937–87* (US Department of the Interior, Fish and Wildlife Service, 1987), 4.

4. Ibid.

5. Ibid.

6. Ibid.

7. Ibid., 8.

8. Ibid., 11.

9. Ibid.

10. Ibid.

11. Ibid.

12. Fannye Cooke to P. W. Allen, 20 July 1934, MMNS.

13. Cook to Allen, 13 August 1934, MMNS.

14. Cook to Allen, September 1934, MMNS.

15. Fannye Cook, "History of Our Wildlife Museum," *Mississippi Game and Fish*, June 1957, 8.

16. Eudora Welty, *One Time, One Place* (New York: Random House, 1975), dust jacket.

17. US census, 1940, ED 25–15A, page 1A, line 20.

18. Suzanne Marrs, *Eudora Welty* (Orlando: Harcourt, 2005), 52.

19. Fannye Cook, Application document, 1936, Plant and Animal Survey, 651.35, RG 69, National Archives and Records Administration, College Park, MD.

20. Cook to Bartsch, 18 April 1936, Smithsonian Institution Archives.

21. Halla Jo Ellis, interview by author, 23 June 2014.

22. "State Game Program in 'Reel' Style," *Jackson Daily News*, 26 Sept. 1937.

23. Cook, Application document.

24. Rehder to Cook, 3 April 1937, Folder Cook, Fannye, Box 8, Collection no. 73, Smithsonian Institution Archives.

25. Fannye Cook, "Mississippi Plant and Animal Survey," *Journal of the Mississippi Academy of Science* 2 (1940): 82–85.

26. Ibid., 82.

27. Ibid., 83.

28. Fannye Cook, report, February 1939, RG 69, National Archives, College Park, MD.

29. Turcotte, "MMNS Celebrates First 50 Years."

30. Cook, "Mississippi Plant and Animal Survey," 85.

31. Fannye Cook and Vivian Cook, *Plant and Animal Survey Project for Mississippi: Final Report for the WPA Plant and Animal Survey Project*, OP 665-62-3-266, WP 5958, February 6, 1939–September 15, 1940 (Jackson: Mississippi Academy of Sciences, 1940), 2.

32. Anonymous biographical sketch and images of paintings by Maud K. Lilly, private collection of her granddaughter Cheryl Simmons.

33. Sammy Ray, telephone interview by author, 17 October 2012; Rory Doyle, "WWII Vet Thankful for Miss. Delta Life," *Bolivar Commercial*, 10 October 2012.

34. John Turcotte, email to author, 15 October 2010.

35. Turcotte and Watts, *Birds of Mississippi*, 9.

36. Cook and Cook, *Plant and Animal Survey*.

37. Cook, "Mississippi Plant and Animal Survey."

38. Cook, "History of Our Wildlife Museum," 8.

39. Ibid.

40. Ibid., 9.

41. Ibid., 11.

42. Ibid., 9.

43. Ibid.

44. Fannye Cook, "Down-Town Museum Becomes One of Show Places," *Mississippi Game and Fish*, March 1939, 2.

Seven. Work Continues in the War Years, 1941–45

1. Marrs, *Eudora Welty*, 80.

2. Eudora Welty, "A Still Moment," in *The Wide Net and Other Stories* (New York: Harcourt, Brace and Company, 1943), 76.

3. Ibid., 81.

4. Ibid., 82.

5. Ibid., 86.

6. Ibid., 88.

7. Ibid., 91.

8. Marrs, *Eudora Welty*, 88.

9. Eudora Welty, "The Wide Net," in *The Wide Net*, 46.

10. Julia Eichelberger, ed. *Tell about Night Flowers: Eudora Welty's Gardening Letters, 1940–1949* (Jackson: University Press of Mississippi, 2013), 66.

11. Marrs, *Eudora Welty*, 99–100.

12. Eudora Welty to John Robinson, 22 February 1944, MDAH.

13. Ibid., 28 March 1944.

14. Margaret Millar, *The Birds and Beasts Were There* (Santa Barbara: Capra Press, 1967).

15. Ibid., 26.

16. Welty to Margaret Millar, 5 December 1971, MDAH.

17. Patti Carr Black, interview by author, 24 May 2013.

18. Cook to Bartsch, 1942, Folder Cook, Fannye, Box 8, Collection no. 73, Smithsonian Institution Archives.

19. Ibid., 1943.

20. Bartsch to Cook, 29 October 1945, Folder Cook, Fannye, Box 8, Collection no. 73, Smithsonian Institution Archives.

21. Fannye Cook, *Fur Resources of Mississippi* (Jackson: Mississippi Game and Fish Commission, 1945), 1.

22. Bartsch to Cook, 27 November 1945, Folder Cook, Fannye, Box 8, Collection no. 73, Smithsonian Institution Archives.

Eight. War's End, 1945–49

1. Eudora Welty to John Robinson, 22 May 1947, MDAH.

2. Eudora Welty to Margaret Millar, 5 Dec. 1971, MDAH.

3. Pruitt, "Best of All Breathing."

4. Ibid.

5. Ibid.

6. Becker, "Ladies Afield," 107.

7. Roger Conant to Fannye Cook, 9 May 1945, Fannye Cook papers, MDAH. All subsequent Cook-Conant correspondence can be found in this collection.

8. Cook to Conant, 15 May 1945.

9. Conant to Cook, 16 July 1946.

10. Cook to Conant, 23 July 1946.

11. Conant to Cook, 27 July 1946.

12. Cook to Conant, 30 July 1946.

13. Conant to Cook, 17 August 1946.

14. Cook to Conant, 27 August 1946.

15. Cook to Conant, 15 May 1948.

16. Cook to Conant, 16 August 1948.

17. Conant to Cook, 23 August 1948.

18. Conant to Cook, 27 December 1949.

19. Roger Conant, "A Review of the Water Snakes of the Genus *Natrix* in Mexico," *Bulletin of the American Museum of Natural History* 142, no. 1 (1969), 23.

20. Ibid., 9.

21. Samuel Hildebrand (1883–1949) was a famous author of several books, including *The Fishes of the Fresh Water of Panama*; it is possible that Cook met him while she was in Panama; according to Steve Ross in Inland Fishes of Mississippi, Hildebrand traveled in Mississippi to collect fish at the request of the Game and Fish Commission—that is, of Fannye Cook.

22. Fannye Cook to S. F. Hildebrand, 12 June 1945, Folder 2, Box 6, Collection no. 234, Smithsonian Institution Archives.

23. Fannye Cook to Leonard P. Schultz, 20 June 1945, Folder 2, Box 6, Collection no. 234, Smithsonian Institution Archives.

24. Cook to Hildebrand, 4 March 1948, Folder 2, Box 6, Collection no. 234, Smithsonian Institution Archives.

25. Ibid.

26. Harald A. Rehder to Fannye Cook, 19 Apr. 1948, Folder Cook, Fannye, Box 8, Collection no. 73, Smithsonian Institution Archives.

27. Pruitt, "Best of All Breathing."

28. Ibid.

29. Ibid.

30. John Turcotte, email to author, 15 October 2010.

31. Ibid.

32. Eudora Welty to Margaret Millar, 5 December 1971, MDAH.

33. Ibid.

Nine. Directing, Collecting, Organizing, and Publishing in the 1950s

1. Bill Cook, interview by author, 3 August 2011, Jackson.

2. "Museum Lady, Crusader for Conservation, Serves State," *Jackson Daily News*, 15 October 1953, Sect. 2, p. 5.

3. Cook correspondence, 1950s, Folder 2, Box 6, Collection no. 234, Smithsonian Institution Archives.

4. Eudora Welty to Mary Louise Aswell, 1955, MDAH.

5. Bettye Tucker, "Museum Director Has Studied Nature Most of Her Life," *Jackson Daily News*, 5 August 1958.

6. William Bizzell, interview by author, 30 September 2013.

7. Hartfield and Huffman, "Fannye A. Cook."

8. Fannye Cook, "History of Our Wildlife Museum," 9.

9. John Turcotte, email to author, 15 October 2010.

10. Ibid.

11. Ibid.

12. Interview with Patti Carr Black by author, 24 May 2013.

13. Libby Hartfield, email to author, 13 April 2014.

14. William Bizzell, interview by author, 20 August 2014.

15. John Turcotte, interview by author, 3 August 2011.

16. John Turcotte, email to author, 15 October 2010.

17. Sam Gore, interview by author, n.d.

18. Pruitt, "Best of All Breathing."

19. Ibid.

20. William Jenkins, *Mississippi United Methodist Churches: 200 Years of Heritage and Hope*, Franklin, TN: Providence House, 1998, 6.

21. Morelle H. Wells, memoir, *Mississippi Annual Conference Journal*, 1989, 414.

22. Pruitt, "Best of All Breathing."

23. Ibid.

24. Ibid.

Ten. The Work Goes On, 1959

1. Pruitt, "Best of All Breathing."

2. "Miss Fannye Cook Publishes New Book 'Fresh Water Fishes in Mississippi,'" *Crystal Springs Meteor*, 4 August 1960.

3. Ibid.

4. Pruitt, "Best of All Breathing."

Eleven. The 1960s and the Last Walk

1. Pruitt, "Best of All Breathing."

2. Ibid.

3. B. E. Gandy, "In Memoriam," 10.

4. "Miss Cook Rites Today," *Jackson Clarion-Ledger*, 2 May 1964.

5. *Jackson Daily News*, 30 March 1967, 5.

6. Elizabeth "Bebe" Wolfe, interview by Libby Hartfield, 19 June 2016.

7. Pruitt, "Best of All Breathing."

8. Ibid.

9. Ibid.

10. "Visit Us," Mississippi Museum of Natural Science, http://www.mdwfp.com/see-visit/about-us.aspx.

11. Pruitt, "Best of All Breathing."

Bibliography

Selected Works by Fannye Cook

"Down-Town Museum Becomes One of Show Places." *Mississippi Game and Fish*, March 1939.

"Mississippi Plant and Animal Survey." *Journal of the Mississippi Academy of Sciences* 2 (1940): 82–85.

Plant and Animal Survey Project for Mississippi: Final Report for the WPA Plant and Animal Survey Project. With Vivian Cook. OP 665-62-3-266. WP 5958. February 6, 1939–September 15, 1940. Jackson: Mississippi Academy of Sciences, 1940.

Research and Investigation of Wildlife in Mississippi. With R. M. Freeman and W. H. Turcotte. Jackson: Mississippi Game and Fish Commission, 1941.

Alligators and Lizards of Mississippi. Survey bulletin. Jackson: Mississippi Game and Fish Commission, 1942.

Research and Investigation of Wildlife in Mississippi. With W. H. Turcotte. Jackson: Mississippi Game and Fish Commission, 1942.

Game Animals of Mississippi. Survey bulletin. Jackson: Mississippi Game and Fish Commission, 1943.

Game Birds in Mississippi. Survey bulletin. Jackson: Mississippi Game and Fish Commission, 1943.

Snakes of Mississippi. Survey bulletin. Jackson: Mississippi Game and Fish Commission, 1943.

Fur Resources of Mississippi. Survey bulletin. Jackson: Mississippi Game and Fish Commission, 1945.

"History of Our Wildlife Museum." *Mississippi Game and Fish*, June 1957.

Early History and Trends in Mississippi Freshwater Fisheries. Survey bulletin. Jackson: Mississippi Game and Fish Commission, 1958.

Freshwater Fishes in Mississippi. Jackson: Mississippi Game and Fish Commission, 1959.

Salamanders of Mississippi. Survey bulletin. Jackson: Mississippi Game and Fish Commission, 1957.

Letters

Bartsch, Paul, and Fannye Cook. Letters. Folder Cook, Fannye, Box 8, Collection no. 73, Smithsonian Institution Archives.

Conant, Roger, and Fannye Cook. Fannye Cook papers. Mississippi Museum of Natural Science, Jackson.

Cook, G. M., and Fannye Cook. Fannye Cook papers. Mississippi Museum of Natural Science, Jackson.

Leopold, Aldo, and Fannye Cook. Leopold letters. Mississippi Museum of Natural Science, Jackson

Welty, Eudora. Papers. Jackson: Mississippi Department of Archives and History, Jackson, Mississippi.

Other Sources

Alford, Dorothy Moore. *Reflections and Recognitions: Crystal Springs, Mississippi, 1820–1972.* Published by Dorothy Moore Alford, n.d.

Bartsch, Paul. "Notes on the Heron of the District of Columbia." *Smithsonian* 45 (1903): 104–11.

Becker, Edwin J. "Ladies Afield." *Independent Woman,* April 1946.

"Brave Thinkers." *The Atlantic,* Nov. 2012.

Buchanan, Minor Ferris. *Holt Collier: His Life, His Roosevelt Hunts, and the Origin of the Teddy Bear.* Jackson: Centennial Press, 2002.

Burns, Ken. *The Roosevelts.* Public Broadcasting Service, Sept. 2014. DVD.

Carson, David. "Elizabeth Lee Hazen." In Swain et al., *Mississippi Women,* 131–43.

Conant, Roger. "A Review of Water Snakes of the Genus *Natrix* in Mexico." *Bulletin of the American Museum of Natural History* 142, no.1 (1969).

Cook, Fannye. "Annual Report of Executive Secretary." Mississippi Association for the Conservation of Wild Life. 14 July 1928. Mississippi Museum of Natural Science, Jackson.

———. "Annual Report of Executive Secretary." Mississippi Association for the Conservation of Wild Life. 19 July 1929. Mississippi Museum of Natural Science, Jackson.

———. Application document. 1936. Plant and Animal Survey, 651.35, RG 69, National Archives and Records Administration, College Park, MD.

———"Application for Position of Teacher." The Panama Canal, Division of Schools, 16 July 1915. National Personnel Records Center, Saint Louis.

———. Papers. Collection nos. 73 (Box 8) and 234 (Box 6), Smithsonian Institution Archives, Washington, DC.

———. Papers. Archive Collection. Mississippi Museum of Natural Science, Jackson.

———. "Prospectus of the Mississippi Association for the Conservation of Wild Life." In Leopold, *Report on a Game Survey,* 80.

Cook family genealogical charts. Mississippi Museum of Natural Science. Jackson.

Cook, Katherine M. *Public Education in the Panama Canal Zone.* US Department of the Interior, Office of Education, Bulletin 139, No. 8.

Crystal Springs' Centennial Celebration: 1858–1958. Crystal Springs: Meteor, 1958.

"Darwin in the House." *Smithsonian*, February 2013, 60–67.

Doyle, Rory. "WWII Vet Thankful for Miss. Delta Life." *Bolivar Commercial*, 10 October 2012.

Eichelberger, Julia, ed. *Tell about Night Flowers: Eudora Welty's Gardening Letters, 1940–1949.* Jackson: University Press of Mississippi, 2013.

Furmansky, Dyana Z. *Rosalie Edge: Hawk of Mercy.* Athens: University of Georgia Press, 2009.

Gandy, B. E. "In Memoriam: Miss Fannye A. Cook." *The Mississippi Kite* 1, no. 1 (May 1965).

General Laws of Mississippi. Meridian, Miss.: Interstate Printers, 1926.

Hamilton, Mary. *Trials of the Earth.* Jackson: University Press of Mississippi, 1992.

Hartfield, Libby, and Alan Huffman. "Fannye A. Cook, Pioneer Conservationist and Scientist, 1889–1964." *Mississippi History Now*, June 2009. http://mshistorynow.mdah.state.ms.us/articles/313/fannye-cook.

Industrial Institute and College Catalog, 1911–1912. Columbus, MS: Mississippi University for Women.

Jenkins, William. *Mississippi United Methodist Churches: 200 Years of Heritage and Hope.* Franklin, TN: Providence House, 1998.

Johnson, Fran Holman. *"The Gift of the Wild Things": The Life of Caroline Dormon.* Lafayette: University of Southwestern Louisiana, 1990.

Leopold, Aldo. *Report on a Game Survey of Mississippi.* 1929, reprinted with maps and correspondence, Jackson, Mississippi Museum of Natural Science, 2010.

Lockwood, T. P. "Reminiscences of Old Crystal Springs." In *Crystal Springs' Centennial Celebration: 1858–1958.* Crystal Springs: Meteor, 1958.

Marrs, Suzanne. "En Route to *A Curtain of Green*," in Swain et al., *Mississippi Women*, 181–95.

———. *Eudora Welty.* Orlando: Harcourt, 2005.

Meh Lady. Columbus, MS: Industrial Institute and College, 1911–12.

Millar, Margaret. *The Birds and Beasts Were There.* Santa Barbara: Capra Press, 1967.

"Miss Cook Rites Today." *Jackson Clarion-Ledger*, 2 May 1964.

"Miss Fannye Cook Publishes New Book 'Fresh Water Fishes in Mississippi.'" *Crystal Springs Meteor*, 4 August 1960.

Mississippi House of Representatives. *Journal of the House of Representatives of the State of Mississippi.* Jackson: Hederman Brothers, 1932.

Mississippi Senate. *Journal of the Senate of the State of Mississippi.* Jackson: Hederman Brothers, 1932.

Mitchell, Dennis. *A New History of Mississippi.* Jackson: University Press of Mississippi, 2014.

Muir, John. "The Scenic Route." *Mental Floss*, July–August 2013.

"Museum Lady, Crusader for Conservation, Serves State." *Jackson Daily News*, 15 October 1953, Sect. 2, p. 5.

Panama Canal documents. National Personnel Records Center, Saint Louis.

Pieschel, Bridget Smith, and Stephen Robert Pieschel. *Loyal Daughters: One Hundred Years of Mississippi University for Women 1884–1994.* Jackson: University Press of Mississippi, 1994.

Pruitt, Wiley. "The Best of All Breathing: Hunting and Environmental Change in Mississippi, 1900–1980." Master's thesis, University of Mississippi, December 1991.

Ripley, S. Dillon, and James A. Steed. *Alexander Wetmore, 1886–1978: A Biographical Memoir.* Washington, DC: National Academy of Sciences, 1978.

Sanders, Marcie. Papers. Mississippi University for Women Archives, Columbus, Mississippi.

Scott, Anne Firor. "Nellie Nugent Somerville." In *Notable American Women: The Modern Period*, edited by Barbara Sicherman and Carol Hurd Green, 254–56. Cambridge, MA: Belknap Press, 1980.

Scott, Anne Firor, and Andrew MacKay Scott. *One Half the People: The Fight for Woman Suffrage.* Urbana: University of Illinois Press, 1982.

Shawhan, Dorothy. "Minnie Brewer." In Swain et al., *Mississippi Women*, 160–80.

Shawhan, Dorothy, and Martha H. Swain. *Lucy Somerville Howorth: New Deal Lawyer, Politician, and Feminist from the South.* Baton Rouge: Louisiana State University Press, 2006.

"Snap Shots at Home News." *Ladner Wyoming State Journal*, 25 July 1919, 1.

Souder, William. "Angry Bird." *Smithsonian*, September 2014, 64–65.

"State Game Program in 'Reel' Style." *Jackson Daily News*, 26 Sept. 1937.

Swain, Martha. *Ellen S. Woodward: New Deal Advocate for Women.* Jackson: University Press of Mississippi, 1995.

Swain, Martha, Elizabeth Payne, and Marjorie Spruill, eds. *Mississippi Women: Their Histories, Their Lives*, vol. 1. Athens: University of Georgia Press, 2003.

Treasury Department documents. National Personnel Records Center, Saint Louis.

Tucker, Bettye. "Museum Director Has Studied Nature Most of Her Life." *Jackson Daily News*, 5 Aug. 1958.

Turcotte, William H. "MMNS Celebrates First 50 Years." *Mississippi Museum of Natural Science Newsletter* 2, no. 1 (1983).

Turcotte, William H., and David L. Watts. *Birds of Mississippi.* Jackson: University Press of Mississippi, 1999.

University Bulletin. Washington, DC: George Washington University, 1923–24.

"Visit Us," Mississippi Museum of Natural Science, http://www.mdwfp.com/see-visit/about-us.aspx.

Wells, Morelle H. Memoir. *Mississippi Annual Conference Journal*, 1989.

Welty, Eudora. *One Time, One Place.* New York: Random House, 1975.

———. *The Wide Net and Other Stories.* New York: Harcourt, Brace and Company, 1943.

Williamson, Lonnie. *Restoring America's Wildlife, 1937–87.* US Department of the Interior, Fish and Wildlife Service, 1987.

"Woman Nature Student Sees Success as Near." *Jackson Daily News*, August 4, 1929.

Woodward, Calvin. "IRS Seems Past Its Glory Days." *Jackson Clarion Ledger*, 2 June 2013.

Wyoming Department of Education. *Wyoming Education Directory, 1917–1918.* Cheyenne: Wyoming Department of Education, 1917.

Index

Page numbers in **bold** refer to illustrations.